The HEART OF THE AMISH COOKBOOK

180 Traditional Amish Recipes

BARBOUR PUBLISHING

Print ISBN 979-8-89151-213-9

Edited by Rebecca Germany.

Cover design by Greg Jackson, Thinkpen Design

Unless otherwise noted, cover and interior Amish photography © J.D. Schrock
Amish photography on pages 53, 81, 116, 126 © Unsplash
Food photography provided by Shutterstock.

Published by Barbour Publishing, Inc., 1810 Barbour Drive, Uhrichsville, OH 44683, www.barbourbooks.com

Our mission is to inspire the world with the life-changing message of the Bible.

Printed in China.

Introduction

If you are driving down a rural road and come upon a sleek horse pulling a black buggy or see a well-kept farm not connected to electric lines or pass a one-room schoolhouse still in use, you may have found yourself in the heart of Amish country.

There are many communities, small and large, of Anabaptist Christians throughout the United States and Canada that have their roots from European immigrants in the 1700s and 1800s who sought freedom to worship as they chose. The most recognizable communities are the Old Order Amish who adhere to a plain lifestyle, avoid social change, and build strong community bonds.

The Pennsylvania Dutch language they use is a mix of German dialects and English. The foods they traditionally serve also have many German influences.

Good, comforting food is something that draws lots of visitors to Amish communities where Amish-owned bakeries and restaurants serve mouthwatering cuisine. In this cookbook we attempt to highlight many of those favorite recipes as shared by over one hundred Amish cooks as well as authors of Amish romance fiction Anne Blackburne and Mindy Steele.

Labour not for the meat which
perisheth, but for that meat
which endureth unto everlasting
life, which the Son of man
shall give unto you: for him
hath God the Father sealed.
~ JOHN 6:27

THE AMISH KITCHEN

No matter if you're Amish or English, home is where the heart is, and to the Amish, the kitchen is the heart of the home.

An Amish kitchen is spacious with an off-grid, homespun vibe. Light-colored walls present few adornments, but there will almost always be a calendar and clock hanging nearby. Food is prepared under the natural lighting of large windows that allow the sunshine to flood in. Additional lighting is propane or battery-operated hanging lamps as well as the expected oil lamps found in nearly every room. Underfoot, floors are typically constructed of polished wood or tile for easy maintenance.

There is a sturdy wooden table that can seat a large family, but it is also great for doing homework, for sewing, or as additional canning space. Cabinets are also wooden and sturdy and designed for functional efficiency. Hutches, also handcrafted of wood, display cards, wedding invitations, pretty glasswares, and those beloved treasured recipes.

There is always a wood-burning stove. Its multifunctional ability to heat, cook, and bake makes it the most important part of every Amish kitchen. Near at hand for easy use, you'll find the basic utensils such as spoons, spatulas, wire whips, and Rada knives. In cooler weather you'll feel the gentle warmth of its fire from an aluminum or stainless steel fan collecting heat from the stovetop and circulating it throughout the home. More often than not, there's a kettle perched on top for a quick cup of tea or instant coffee.

In addition to wood-burning stoves, there will be a gas stove nearby or in a part of the home many refer to as the "summer kitchen." From single to four burners, they work on mineral spirits, which burns cleaner and safer than kerosene. Specially crafted baker's ovens fit nicely on top.

Without electricity, food is stored in propane refrigerators or freezers, but Old Order Amish and the more conservative communities continue to use ice chests, coolers, or icehouses.

The absence of modern electrical appliances (such as dishwashers, blenders, mixers, and microwaves) hasn't taken away from the exceptional food produced in the Amish home. Instead, you'll find hand-crank or rechargeable battery-operated appliances.

Popcorn is made on the stovetop, and ice cream is hand churned to creamy perfection. There are no Crock-Pots, but large amounts of food (such as wedding chicken or barbecue) are cooked and placed in coolers where they will remain at a safe temperature until served. There are noodle makers, presses—and every home has a King Cutter that at the turn of a crank will slice, dice, and grate everything from potatoes to cucumbers for homemade pickles. Handheld beaters and whips take the place of most conventional mixers, and battery-operated blenders make the best smoothies.

Even without modern appliances, the Amish kitchen remains true to simplicity. The use of fresh, natural ingredients blended with generations of hand-me-down knowledge continues to set a fine table at the end of every day.

MINDY STEELE

Mindy writes Amish romance fiction, drawing inspiration from her Amish neighbors in rural Kentucky.

A PLACE OF HAPPINESS

Home is not a house alone,
It's family and friends
The warmth that kitchen gatherings
And a cup of coffee lends.
It's love and understanding
Blended well with kindness
That fills the heart and makes the home
A place of happiness.

Mrs. Menno Miller, Gallipolis, OH

BREAKING *the* FAST

My voice shalt thou hear in the morning, O LORD; in the morning will I direct my prayer unto thee, and will look up.

~PSALM 5:3

GRANOLA

INGREDIENTS:

- 20 cups quick oats
- 4 cups shredded coconut
- 2 cups brown sugar
- 2 cups maple syrup
- 2 teaspoons cinnamon
- 2 teaspoons salt
- 3 teaspoons baking soda
- 1 cup melted butter
- 8 cups crisp rice cereal
- 2 packages graham crackers, crushed
- 1 pound raisins

INSTRUCTIONS:

1. Preheat oven to 250 degrees.
2. In roaster pan, mix oats, coconut, brown sugar, maple syrup, cinnamon, salt, and baking soda. Drizzle with butter and mix well to coat.
3. Bake for 1½ hours, stirring occasionally.
4. When cooled, mix in cereal, graham crackers, and raisins.

Mrs. Joseph Miller, *Navarre, OH*

PUMPKIN SEED AND FLAX GRANOLA

INGREDIENTS:

3 cups rolled oats
1½ cups almond flour or fresh ground whole grain flour
½ cup maple syrup
¼ cup water
¼ cup coconut oil
½ cup pumpkin seeds
¼ cup sunflower seeds
2 tablespoons chia seeds
1 cup fine shredded coconut
½ teaspoon salt
½ teaspoon cinnamon

INSTRUCTIONS:

1. Preheat oven to 200 degrees.
2. In bowl, mix all ingredients and spread on baking sheets.
3. Toast at 200 degrees until fully dry.
4. Store in airtight container.

Anna M. Weaver, *Mertztown, PA*

GRAPE NUTS CEREAL

INGREDIENTS:

6 cups whole wheat flour
½ teaspoon salt
½ cup butter
1 cup honey
1 cup maple syrup
1 tablespoon vanilla
½ teaspoon maple flavoring
2 cups sour milk (or add 1 tablespoon vinegar to sweet milk) or buttermilk
½ tablespoon baking soda

INSTRUCTIONS:

1. Preheat oven to 350 degrees.
2. In mixing bowl, combine flour and salt; set aside.
3. In saucepan, melt butter. Add honey and maple syrup, stirring. Add vanilla, maple flavoring, milk, and baking soda.
4. Add melted mixture to flour, stirring well.
5. Pour into 9x13-inch cake pan.
6. Bake at 350 degrees for 30 minutes until center springs back. Cool completely.
7. Crumble finely. Spread on baking sheet.
8. Dry in a 250 to 275 degree oven for 60 to 90 minutes, stirring often until dry.
9. Store in airtight container.

Elizabeth Y. Miller, *Middlefield, OH*

GRANOLA BARS

INGREDIENTS:

- 2 cups quick oats
- 2 cups old-fashioned oats
- 1 cup unsweetened coconut
- ½ cup dried cranberries or raisins
- ½ cup slivered almonds
- 1 cup dark chocolate or sugar-free chips
- ¼ cup honey
- ¼ cup butter
- ¼ cup olive oil
- ¼ cup maple syrup
- ¾ cup peanut butter
- 2 teaspoons vanilla

INSTRUCTIONS:

1. In large bowl, combine quick oats, old-fashioned oats, coconut, cranberries, almonds, and chocolate chips.
2. In saucepan, bring honey, butter, olive oil, maple syrup, and peanut butter to a boil. Add vanilla.
3. Pour over dry ingredients. Mix well and press into 9x13-inch pan.
4. Cool before cutting. Store in a cool, dry place.

Iva Yoder, *Goshen, IN*

PROTEIN BARS

INGREDIENTS:

1¼ cups peanut butter
½ cup coconut oil
½ cup white grape juice or honey
2 tablespoons water
3 cups oatmeal
1 cup unsweetened coconut
½ cup flaxseed
¼ cup chia seeds
2 scoops protein powder
1 cup unsweetened chocolate chips

INSTRUCTIONS:

1. In saucepan, heat peanut butter, oil, grape juice, and water until warm enough to mix well. Stir in oatmeal, coconut, flaxseed, chia seeds, protein power, and chocolate chips.
2. Spread into pan and cut into bars.

Katie Yoder, *Utica, OH*

HEALTHY NO-BAKE ENERGY BITES

INGREDIENTS:

- 1 cup old-fashioned oats
- 3 tablespoons unsweetened cocoa powder
- ½ cup ground flaxseed
- ⅓ cup shredded coconut
- ⅓ cup dried cranberries
- 1 tablespoon chia seeds
- ¼ cup chocolate chips
- Dash salt
- ½ cup peanut butter
- ⅓ cup honey
- 2 tablespoons coconut oil or butter
- ½ teaspoon vanilla
- ⅓ cup chopped almonds or walnuts, sesame seeds, or sunflower seeds
- Coconut, finely chopped (optional)

INSTRUCTIONS:

1. In bowl, mix oats, cocoa powder, flaxseed, coconut, cranberries, chia seeds, chocolate chips, and salt.
2. Stir in peanut butter, honey, coconut oil, and vanilla until all is well coated.
3. Mix in nuts or seeds.
4. Roll into balls.
5. Roll balls in coconut if desired.

Susan M. Schlabach, *Dayton, PA*

BLUEBERRY SMOOTHIE

INGREDIENTS:

- 1 cup fresh blueberries
- 1 banana
- ¼ cup yogurt
- ¼ cup milk
- ½ cup pineapple or orange juice
- Pinch cinnamon

INSTRUCTIONS:

In blender, mix all together until smooth. Serve immediately.

Makes 1 serving.

Barbie Stoltzfoos, *Oxford, PA*

YOGURT PARFAIT

INGREDIENTS:

- 2½ cups granola
- 1 (8 ounce) package cream cheese, softened
- ½ cup sour cream
- 4 cups yogurt
- 2 tablespoons lemon juice
- 1 (8 ounce) carton whipped topping
- Fresh fruit

INSTRUCTIONS:

1. In 9x13 plastic or glass container, level granola over the bottom.
2. In bowl, mix cream cheese, sour cream, yogurt, lemon juice, and whipped topping.
3. Spread mixture over granola.
4. Top with desired choice and amount of fruit.

Barbara D. Zook, *Dalton, OH*

MORNING GLORY MUFFINS

INGREDIENTS:

⅔ cup olive oil
3 eggs
1 cup Sucanat or sugar
2 teaspoons baking soda
2 teaspoons cinnamon
½ teaspoon salt
½ cup milk
2 cups grated carrot
½ cup raisins
½ cup chopped nuts
½ cup shredded coconut
1 apple, grated
2 cups whole wheat flour

INSTRUCTIONS:

1. Preheat oven to 350 degrees.
2. In mixing bowl, blend all ingredients until well combined.
3. Spoon into greased or lined muffin tins.
4. Bake for 20 minutes.

Joann Miller, *Fredericktown, OH*

BLUEBERRY MUFFINS

This recipe makes a lot for an event or bake sale.

MUFFIN INGREDIENTS:

- 3 sticks plus 1 tablespoon butter, softened
- 3⅓ cups sugar
- 5 eggs
- 5 cups sour cream
- 5 teaspoons vanilla
- 7½ cups flour
- 3¾ teaspoons baking soda
- 3¾ teaspoons baking powder
- ¼ teaspoon salt
- 1 tablespoon butter, softened
- Blueberries, fresh or frozen

STREUSEL INGREDIENTS:

- 3¾ cups flour
- 5 cups sugar
- 1 cup butter, softened

MUFFIN INSTRUCTIONS:

1. Preheat oven to 350 degrees.
2. In bowl, cream butter with sugar. Add eggs. Add sour cream and vanilla. Mix in flour, baking soda, baking powder, salt, and 1 tablespoon butter.
3. Gently mix in blueberries in the amount you prefer.
4. Divide batter into lined muffin tins.
5. Top with streusel.
6. Bake for 25 to 30 minutes until toothpick comes out clean.

STREUSEL INSTRUCTIONS:

Mix all ingredients together until crumbly.

Glenda K. Schwartz, *Milford, IN*

PUMPKIN APPLE STREUSEL MUFFINS

MUFFIN INGREDIENTS:

- 2 eggs
- ¾ cup cooked pumpkin
- ½ cup vegetable oil
- 2½ cups flour
- 2 cups sugar
- 1 teaspoon cinnamon
- 1 teaspoon baking soda
- ½ teaspoon salt
- 2 cups chopped apples

TOPPING INGREDIENTS:

- 2 tablespoons flour
- ¼ cup sugar
- ½ teaspoon cinnamon
- 2 teaspoons butter, softened

MUFFIN INSTRUCTIONS:

1. Preheat oven to 350 degrees.
2. Grease 36 muffin tin holes.
3. In mixing bowl, beat eggs, pumpkin, and oil. Add flour, sugar, cinnamon, baking soda, and salt. Stir in apples.
4. Fill greased muffin tins about ¾ full.
5. Combine topping ingredients and sprinkle on top.
6. Bake for 35 minutes or until done.

TOPPING INSTRUCTIONS:

Mix all ingredients together until crumbly.

Katie Gingerich, *Dalton, OH*

WALNUT WONDER COFFEE CAKE

CAKE INGREDIENTS:

- 1 cup butter, melted
- 1 cup brown sugar
- 2 eggs
- 1 teaspoon vanilla
- ½ teaspoon salt
- 1 teaspoon baking soda
- 1 teaspoon baking powder
- 1 cup milk
- 2½ cups flour

TOPPING INGREDIENTS:

- ½ cup brown sugar
- ¼ cup sugar
- 1 teaspoon cinnamon
- 1 cup chopped walnuts

FILLING INGREDIENTS:

- 3 cups powdered sugar
- 1 cup shortening
- 1 teaspoon vanilla
- 3 egg whites, beaten stiff

CAKE INSTRUCTIONS:

1. Preheat oven to 325 degrees.
2. In mixing bowl, cream butter and brown sugar together. Add eggs. Add vanilla, salt, baking soda, baking powder, milk, and flour, mixing until well combined.
3. Spread into 2 greased 9-inch round pans.

TOPPING INSTRUCTIONS:

1. In bowl, stir all ingredients together and sprinkle on top of cake batter in both pans.
2. Bake for 20 to 25 minutes or until cake tests done.
3. Cool and remove cakes from pans to cool completely.

FILLING INSTRUCTIONS:

1. In bowl, cream together powdered sugar and shortening. Add vanilla and stiff egg whites.
2. Spread filling on top of one cake. Set other cake on top of filling.

Lizzie Hostetler, *Polk, OH*

BAKED OATMEAL

INGREDIENTS:

- ½ cup maple syrup
- ½ cup butter, melted
- 2 eggs
- 3 cups oatmeal
- 2 teaspoons baking powder
- 1 teaspoon salt
- ½ cup milk
- 2 cups chopped apples
- 1 teaspoon nutmeg

INSTRUCTIONS:

1. Preheat oven to 350 degrees.
2. In bowl, mix all ingredients together and stir well until blended.
3. Pour into greased loaf pan.
4. Bake for 30 minutes.
5. To serve, layer baked oatmeal, blueberries, strawberries, yogurt, and granola.

Makes 7 servings.

Lena Troyer, *Redding, IA*

CORNMEAL MUSH

INGREDIENTS:

- 3 cups water
- 1 cup cold water
- 1 cup cornmeal
- 2 teaspoons salt

INSTRUCTIONS:

1. In deep saucepan, heat 3 cups water to boiling.
2. In bowl, mix cold water, cornmeal, and salt. Add to boiling water, stirring constantly until it reaches a full boil.
3. Cover and cook for 20 minutes.
4. Pour into a loaf pan or two. Let cool completely.
5. Slice and fry in oil.
6. Serve with maple syrup.

Mrs. Joseph Miller, *Navarre, OH*

FLUFFY FRENCH TOAST

INGREDIENTS:

1 egg

1 cup flour

1½ teaspoons sugar

1½ teaspoons brown sugar

½ teaspoon salt

1 cup milk

8 to 10 slices homemade bread

Powdered sugar or cinnamon and sugar mixture

Maple syrup

INSTRUCTIONS:

1. In bowl, beat egg. Add flour, sugar, brown sugar, salt, and milk.
2. Dip bread in mixture until soaked.
3. Deep-fry in oil until golden brown.
4. Sprinkle with powdered sugar or mixture of cinnamon and sugar.
5. Serve with maple syrup.

Mrs. Joseph Miller, *Navarre, OH*

BLUEBERRY FRENCH TOAST

TOAST INGREDIENTS:

- 12 slices bread, cubed
- 2 (8 ounce) packages cream cheese, cubed
- 1 cup blueberries
- 12 eggs
- ½ cup maple syrup
- 1 cup milk

SAUCE INGREDIENTS:

- 1 cup water
- 1 cup sugar
- 2 tablespoons cornstarch
- 1 cup blueberries
- 1 tablespoon butter

TOAST INSTRUCTIONS:

1. Preheat oven to 350 degrees.
2. Put bread in 9x13-inch baking dish. Scatter cubes of cream cheese and blueberries on top.
3. In mixing bowl, beat together eggs, syrup, and milk. Pour over bread.
4. Cover and bake 30 minutes.
5. Uncover and bake another 30 minutes.
6. Serve with sauce.

SAUCE INSTRUCTIONS:

1. In saucepan, cook water, sugar, and cornstarch for 3 minutes.
2. Add blueberries and butter, stirring until butter melts.

Anna Swartzentruber, *West Salem, OH*

BREAKFAST OMELET SANDWICHES

INGREDIENTS:

16 slices toasted and buttered bread
8 slices cheese
1 pound chipped ham
6 eggs
3 cups milk
½ teaspoon mustard
½ teaspoon salt
1 cup crushed cornflakes
½ cup melted butter

INSTRUCTIONS:

1. Make 8 sandwiches with bread, cheese, and ham. Set single layer in greased pan.
2. In bowl, blend eggs, milk, mustard, and salt. Pour over sandwiches.
3. Refrigerate overnight.
4. In the morning, mix cornflakes and butter. Sprinkle over top.
5. Bake at 350 degrees for 1 hour.

Makes 8 big servings.

Katie Swartzentruber, *Polk, OH*

GLUTEN-FREE PANCAKES

INGREDIENTS:

2 eggs, separated
¼ cup oil
1 teaspoon salt
2 teaspoons baking powder
1½ cups oatmeal
½ cup cornmeal
1½ cups milk

INSTRUCTIONS:

1. In blender, mix egg yolks, oil, salt, baking powder, oatmeal, cornmeal, and milk.
2. In bowl, beat egg whites until stiff. Add mixture and stir into egg whites.
3. Fry in hot oiled skillet.

Esther Martin, *Fleetwood, PA*

FLANNEL PANCAKES

PANCAKE INGREDIENTS:

- 2 cups flour
- 6 teaspoons baking powder
- 2 tablespoons sugar
- 2 eggs, beaten
- 1 tablespoon melted butter
- ¼ teaspoon salt
- Milk

HOMEMADE SYRUP INGREDIENTS:

- 1 cup sugar
- 1 cup brown sugar
- 1 cup water
- 1 teaspoon maple flavoring

PANCAKE INSTRUCTIONS:

1. In bowl, mix flour, baking powder, and sugar. Mix in eggs, butter, and salt. Add just enough milk to make a fairly thin batter.
2. Spoon onto hot, lightly greased griddle and fry both sides until lightly browned.
3. Serve with maple syrup or meat gravy.

HOMEMADE SYRUP INSTRUCTIONS:

1. In saucepan, combine sugar, brown sugar, and water; bring to a boil for 3 to 4 minutes.
2. Add maple flavoring.

Mattie J. Gingerich, *Dalton, OH*

WHOLE WHEAT PANCAKES

PANCAKE INGREDIENTS:

- 1 egg
- 1 cup buttermilk
- 2 tablespoons vegetable oil
- 1 cup whole wheat flour
- ½ teaspoon salt
- ½ teaspoon baking soda
- 1 teaspoon baking powder
- 1 teaspoon vanilla

Note: If you don't have buttermilk, put 1 tablespoon vinegar in a cup measuring cup then fill with milk.

SAUCE INGREDIENTS:

- 1 cup brown sugar
- 2 cups water
- ½ cup butter
- 1 heaping tablespoon flour
- Maple flavoring

PANCAKE INSTRUCTIONS:

1. In bowl, beat all ingredients together to combine into a batter.
2. Pour by spoonfuls onto greased skillet and fry both sides.

SAUCE INSTRUCTIONS:

In saucepan, combine all ingredients and bring to a boil while stirring. When a boil is reached, it is ready to serve.

Mrs. Joseph Miller, *Navarre, OH*

DUTCH BREAKFAST PANCAKES

INGREDIENTS:

4 tablespoons butter

2 medium apples, peeled and thinly sliced

¾ cup milk

1 teaspoon almond extract

½ teaspoon salt

4 eggs

2 teaspoons vanilla

¾ cup fresh ground whole wheat flour

Cinnamon

INSTRUCTIONS:

1. Preheat oven to 400 degrees.
2. Spray 2 (8 or 9 inch) pans lightly with cooking oil.
3. Put 2 tablespoons butter in each pan and place in oven to melt butter.
4. Remove pans and swirl to coat bottoms and sides with butter.
5. Layer apples evenly in pans and set aside.
6. In bowl, combine milk, almond extract, salt, eggs, vanilla, and flour and beat well.
7. Divide batter between pans. Sprinkle cinnamon over top.
8. Bake under a watchful eye for 20 minutes until puffed up and lightly browned. Can lower temperature to 300 degrees if another 5 minutes are needed.
9. Serve with maple syrup.

Joann Miller, *Fredericktown, OH*

BREAKFAST TARTS

INGREDIENTS:

- 6 ounces cream cheese, softened
- 2 tablespoons milk
- 2 eggs
- ½ cup shredded Colby cheese
- 2 tablespoons diced green pepper
- 1 tablespoon finely chopped onion
- 1 tube crescent roll dough
- 5 strips bacon, cooked and crumbled

INSTRUCTIONS:

1. Preheat oven to 375 degrees.
2. In small bowl, beat cream cheese and milk until smooth. Add eggs, cheese, green pepper, and onion, mixing well.
3. Separate dough into 8 triangles. Press into bottom and up sides of greased muffin cups.
4. Take half the bacon and divide into bottoms of cups.
5. Divide egg mixture over bacon in each cup.
6. Top with remaining bacon.
7. Bake for 18 to 22 minutes, until knife inserted comes out clean.
8. Serve warm.

Barbara Coblentz, *Greenfield, OH*

BREAKFAST SKILLET CASSEROLE

INGREDIENTS:

1 pound bulk sausage
¾ cup cubed ham
½ cup chopped bacon
¼ cup chopped red pepper
¼ cup chopped green pepper
Mushroom pieces
1 teaspoon salt
½ teaspoon onion salt
14 eggs
1⅓ cups milk
Velveeta or American cheese slices or shredded cheddar cheese

INSTRUCTIONS:

1. In skillet, brown sausage, ham, bacon, red pepper, green pepper, mushrooms, salt, and onion salt.
2. In bowl, beat eggs with milk. Add to sausage and stir-fry until done.
3. Top with cheese.

Mrs. Joseph Miller, *Navarre, OH*

SAUSAGE GRAVY

INGREDIENTS:

2 pounds bulk sausage
1¼ cups flour
¼ cup butter
2 quarts milk
Salt to taste
Seasoned salt to taste
Pepper to taste

INSTRUCTIONS:

1. In large skillet, brown sausage and ¼ cup flour in butter.
2. Mix in 1 cup flour. Slowly add milk and stir while it cooks to thicken. Simmer over low heat to develop rich flavor.
3. Add more milk to reach desired consistency.
4. Season to taste with salt, seasoned salt, and pepper.
5. Serve over biscuits.

Ella E. Shetler, *West Salem, OH*

BREAKFAST WRAPS

INGREDIENTS:

½ pound bacon, chopped, or sausage
¼ cup diced green pepper
1 dozen eggs
Salt and pepper to taste
Velveeta cheese
Soft tortilla wraps
Salsa

INSTRUCTIONS:

1. In skillet, fry bacon with peppers until peppers are softened. Add eggs, stirring as they cook.
2. Season to taste with salt and pepper.
3. When eggs are almost done, add cheese to your taste. Stir until cheese is melted.
4. Serve egg mixture on tortilla wraps. We like to add salsa too.

Rebecca Byler, *Spartansburg, PA*

BREAKFAST PIZZA

INGREDIENTS:

- 1½ cups flour
- ¾ teaspoon salt
- 2 teaspoons baking powder
- 3 tablespoons shortening
- ¾ cup milk
- 9 eggs
- Bacon, fried and crumbled
- Ham, diced
- 1 can cream of mushroom soup
- 1 can cream of chicken soup
- Potatoes, cooked and shredded
- Cheese, shredded

INSTRUCTIONS:

1. Preheat oven to 350 degrees.
2. In bowl, blend flour, salt, and baking powder. Cut in shortening until crumbly. Slowly mix in milk to form dough.
3. Spread dough on greased 11x15-inch pan.
4. Bake for 10 minutes.
5. Meanwhile, in skillet, cook eggs, stirring to scramble. Spread over crust.
6. Top with bacon and ham.
7. In bowl, mix mushroom and chicken soups with potatoes. Spread over meat.
8. Top with cheese.
9. Bake 10 to 15 minutes to heat through.

Ella Yoder, *Homerville, OH*

PANCAKE PIZZA

INGREDIENTS:

- 2 cups pancake batter
- 1 dozen eggs
- Oil or butter
- Cheese, shredded
- 2 cups sausage gravy
- 1 pound bacon, fried and crumbled (optional)
- Maple syrup

INSTRUCTIONS:

1. Preheat oven to 400 degrees.
2. Pour pancake batter into greased and floured 9x13-inch pan. Bake for 14 minutes or until done.
3. In skillet, scramble eggs in some oil or butter.
4. Layer eggs onto pancake and sprinkle with cheese.
5. Heat gravy through and pour over eggs.
6. Sprinkle with bacon.
7. Cut into squares and serve with maple syrup.

Lori Miller, *Middlefield, OH*

THE WRECK

This is a well-known breakfast at a local Amish restaurant.

INGREDIENTS:

- Biscuit, crumbled
- Meat of choice, fried and chopped (sausage, ham, bacon, etc.)
- Hash brown potatoes, diced or shredded, and fried
- Peppers and onions, sautéed
- Eggs, scrambled
- Cheese, shredded
- Sausage gravy

INSTRUCTIONS:

Layer on your plate ingredients in order given and in amounts of your preference.

Mrs. Anna Raber, *Millersburg, OH*

ROLLING *the* DOUGH

Give us this day our daily bread.

~ Matthew 6:11

MELT-IN-YOUR-MOUTH BISCUITS

INGREDIENTS:

2 cups flour
4 teaspoons baking powder
½ teaspoon cream of tartar
½ teaspoon salt
2 tablespoons sugar
½ cup shortening
⅔ cup milk
1 egg

INSTRUCTIONS:

1. Preheat oven to 450 degrees.
2. Sift together flour, baking powder, cream of tartar, salt, and sugar. Cut in shortening until it resembles coarse meal. Pour milk in slowly. Add egg and stir well.
3. Drop dough by spoonfuls onto cookie sheet.
4. Bake for 10 to 15 minutes.

Ella E. Shetler, *West Salem, OH*

HOMEMADE BISQUICK

INGREDIENTS:

9 cups flour
⅓ cup baking powder
1 tablespoon salt
2 teaspoons cream of tartar
4 tablespoons sugar
1 cup nonfat dry milk (optional)
2 cups shortening

INSTRUCTIONS:

1. In bowl, mix flour, baking powder, salt, cream of tartar, sugar, and dry milk. Cut in shortening until it looks like coarse cornmeal.
2. Store in airtight container.
3. To use: Mix 2 cups Homemade Bisquick with ⅔ cup milk. Shape into biscuits or drop by spoonfuls onto baking sheet. Bake at 375 degrees for 12 to 15 minutes.

Emma Byler, *New Wilmington, PA*

BUTTERHORNS

INGREDIENTS:

1 cup milk, scalded
½ cup shortening
½ cup sugar
1 teaspoon salt
1 tablespoon yeast
3 eggs, beaten
4½ cups flour
Melted butter

INSTRUCTIONS:

1. Scald milk then add shortening, sugar, and salt. Cool to lukewarm.
2. Add yeast, stirring to dissolve.
3. Add eggs and then flour.
4. Knead lightly on floured surface.
5. Put dough into greased bowl. Cover and let rise until doubled.
6. Divide into 3 parts and roll each part into circle. Brush with melted butter.
7. Cut each circle into 12 pie-shaped wedges. Roll up each wedge, starting from wide end, making crescent shape. Put on greased baking sheets, cover, and let rise until very light.
8. Bake at 350 degrees for 10 to 12 minutes until lightly browned. Watch carefully so they do not overbake.
9. Remove from oven and brush tops with butter.
10. These are melt-in-your-mouth delicious!

Makes 3 dozen.

Mrs. Andy (Malinda) Gingerich, *Hartford, KS*

SWEET POTATO BUTTERHORNS

INGREDIENTS:

- 2 tablespoons yeast
- 1 cup water
- 2 cups cooked and mashed sweet potatoes
- ½ cup sugar
- ½ cup butter
- 1 egg, beaten
- 1½ teaspoons salt
- 5 to 5½ cups bread flour
- Melted butter
- Cinnamon-sugar mixture

INSTRUCTIONS:

1. In mixing bowl, dissolve yeast in water. Let sit for 5 minutes.
2. Beat in sweet potatoes, sugar, butter, egg, salt, and 3 cups flour. Mix well.
3. Mix in 2 to 2½ cups flour to make a stiff dough. Mix for 10 minutes.
4. Place dough in greased bowl. Cover and let rise.
5. Divide dough into 3 parts. Roll each part into 12-inch circle.
6. Brush with melted butter and sprinkle with cinnamon and sugar.
7. Cut circle into 12 wedges.
8. Roll each wedge up from widest end. Set on baking sheet with pointed end down.
9. Cover and let rise until double.
10. Bake at 350 degrees for 15 minutes.
11. Serve warm with honey butter.

Joann Miller, *Fredericktown, OH*

BREADSTICKS

INGREDIENTS:

- 1½ cups warm water
- 1 tablespoon yeast
- 1 tablespoon sugar
- 1¼ teaspoons salt
- ¼ cup oil
- 4 cups bread flour
- ¾ cup butter
- 1 teaspoon garlic salt
- 1 tablespoon parsley
- 1 tablespoon Italian seasoning
- Parmesan cheese

INSTRUCTIONS:

1. In bowl, combine water and yeast; dissolve. Add sugar, salt, oil, and flour. Let rise until doubled.
2. Roll dough out and cut into 1-inch strips. Place on cookie sheet.
3. In saucepan, melt butter; add garlic salt, parsley, and Italian seasoning. Spread over dough sticks. Let rise slightly.
4. Bake at 350 degrees for 10 to 15 minutes.
5. Sprinkle with Parmesan cheese while still hot.

Makes 50 sticks.

Lovina Nissley, *Chatham, VA*

30-MINUTE HAMBURGER BUNS

INGREDIENTS:

- 3½ cups warm water
- 1 cup vegetable oil
- ⅓ cup instant yeast
- 3 eggs
- 1 teaspoon salt
- ¾ cup sugar or ½ cup honey
- 10½ cups flour

INSTRUCTIONS:

1. In large mixing bowl, combine water, oil, yeast, eggs, salt, and sugar. Let sit for 15 minutes.
2. Add flour, mixing until dough forms.
3. Shape dough into balls immediately.
4. Set on baking sheets and let rise until doubled in size.
5. Bake at 425 degrees for 10 minutes.

Mrs. Menno Miller, *Gallipolis, OH*

MILLERS
BUGGY
SHOP

GRANDMA'S BREAD

INGREDIENTS:

11 cups flour, divided
3 tablespoons yeast
1 tablespoon salt
4 tablespoons sugar
4½ cups warm water
4 tablespoons melted lard

INSTRUCTIONS:

1. In large bowl, measure 5 cups flour and add yeast, salt, and sugar, mixing well.
2. Add water and lard, mixing well. Add 6 cups flour and mix well.
3. Knead mixture with a little oil on hands. Add additional flour if necessary to make a dough that can be handled.
4. Cover and let rise until doubled.
5. Punch dough down and let rise again.
6. Divide dough into greased bread pans.
7. Bake at 350 degrees for 30 to 40 minutes until done.

Levi and Mary Miller, *Junction City, OH*

BARBARA'S WHITE BREAD

Bread is an everyday staple in most Amish homes. This recipe holds firmness longer than average and is perfect for freezing. My dear friend Barbara made dozens of loaves to send to North Carolina to help feed many without homes after a devastating hurricane and massive flooding. — Mindy Steele

INGREDIENTS:

- 2 cups oatmeal
- ½ cup sugar
- 3 teaspoons salt
- ½ cup lard
- 3 cups hot water
- 3 cups cool water
- 3 tablespoons yeast
- 12 to 15 cups flour

INSTRUCTIONS:

1. In large mixing bowl, mix oatmeal, sugar, salt, lard, and hot water. Let stand 30 minutes.
2. Add cool water until mixture is lukewarm. Then add yeast, blend well, and let sit for 20 minutes.
3. Add flour, 1 cup at a time, until it no longer sticks to fingers. Let rise until double (1 to 1½ hours).
4. Punch down dough and form 6 loaves. Place loaves in greased bread pans. Let rise to double in size.
5. Bake at 350 degrees for 30 minutes until brown.

Barbara Eicher, *Kentucky*

WHOLESOME BREAD

INGREDIENTS:

4½ cups lukewarm water
¾ cup olive oil
½ cup honey
3 tablespoons instant yeast
2 tablespoons lecithin
2 heaping tablespoons vital wheat gluten
1 tablespoon sea salt
12 to 14 cups whole wheat flour

INSTRUCTIONS:

1. Into Bosch or similar mixer, place water, oil, and honey; mix briefly. Add yeast, lecithin, gluten, and salt; mix briefly.
2. Add 6 cups flour. Mix well. Add 5 cups flour. Mix well. Continue adding flour ½ cup at a time while mixer works on low speed until dough starts cleaning side of bowl. Mix for 10 minutes.
3. Let dough sit for 5 minutes.
4. Divide dough into 5 loaves. Shape and fit into greased loaf pans. Prick tops with fork to release air bubbles.
5. Set in oven with pilot light on to rise for 30 minutes.
6. Turn oven on to 350 degrees and bake for 30 to 35 minutes.
7. Let cool on racks for 20 minutes before putting in bags.

Note: Use freshly ground flour for best results.

Anna Swartzentruber, *West Salem, OH*

MULTIGRAIN BREAD

INGREDIENTS:

6 cups warm water
3 eggs
¾ cup sorghum molasses
1 cup olive oil
1 tablespoon apple cider vinegar
2 tablespoons lecithin
½ cup instant potato flakes
4 cups freshly ground whole wheat flour
1 cup quick oats
¾ cup rye flour
¾ cup spelt flour
¾ cup cornmeal
4 tablespoons instant yeast
4 tablespoons vital wheat gluten
4 tablespoons flaxseed meal
6 teaspoons salt
8 cups whole wheat flour

INSTRUCTIONS:

1. Into bowl of mixer (I use Bosch mixer), put warm water, eggs, molasses, oil, vinegar, lecithin, and potato flakes and mix with whisk beater.
2. Meanwhile, measure and mix freshly ground flour, oats, rye flour, spelt flour, cornmeal, yeast, gluten, flaxseed meal, and salt. Add to liquid mixture and whisk for 5 to 10 minutes.
3. Change beater to dough hook.
4. Add 1 cup whole wheat flour every 2 to 3 minutes of mixing until dough leaves side of bowl, adding approximately 8 cups flour total.
5. Dump dough out onto floured surface. Cut into 6 equal pieces. Knead each one a few times.
6. Put each into greased bread pan. Let rise until double.
7. Bake at 350 degrees for 45 minutes.

Anna M. Byler, *Commodore, PA*

HEALTH BREAD

INGREDIENTS:

- 2 cups bran flakes or All Bran cereal
- 2 cups buttermilk
- 4 teaspoons molasses
- 1 cup raisins
- 2 teaspoons baking soda
- 2 cups flour
- ¼ cup sweetener of choice

INSTRUCTIONS:

1. Preheat oven to 350 degrees.
2. In large bowl, combine all ingredients.
3. Pour into large greased loaf pan or 2 small loaf pans.
4. Bake for 45 to 60 minutes.

David C. P. Schwartz, *Galesburg, KS*

TOMATO BREAD

A delicious sandwich bread.

INGREDIENTS:

- 2½ cups water
- 2 cups pizza sauce
- ½ cup sugar
- 2 tablespoons butter
- 1 tablespoon basil
- 1 tablespoon oregano
- 1 tablespoon garlic salt
- 2 tablespoons salt
- ½ cup oil
- 3 tablespoons yeast
- 9 to 10 cups flour

INSTRUCTIONS:

1. In saucepan, gently heat water, pizza sauce, sugar, butter, basil, oregano, garlic salt, and salt to lukewarm. Add oil and yeast.
2. Work in flour, kneading well. Let rise until twice in size.
3. Divide into 4 lightly greased loaf pans and let rise again.
4. Bake at 350 degrees for 30 minutes.

Orla and Alice Petersheim, *Dalton, WI*

PERFECT CORN BREAD

INGREDIENTS:

2 eggs
½ cup canola oil
1 cup milk
1 cup flour
½ cup sugar
4 teaspoons baking powder
¾ teaspoon salt
1 cup yellow cornmeal

INSTRUCTIONS:

1. Preheat oven to 395 degrees and preheat 12-inch cast-iron skillet.
2. In bowl, beat together eggs, oil, and milk.
3. In another bowl, sift together flour, sugar, baking powder, salt, and cornmeal. Mix into wet mixture.
4. Pour into preheated skillet.
5. Bake for approximately 20 minutes.

Mrs. Albert L. Yoder, *Stanwood, MI*

JALAPEÑO CHEESE BREAD

This bread is a good seller and the family loves it too, so we make 8 loaves at a time.

INGREDIENTS:

- 18 cups flour
- 1 cup sugar
- 2 tablespoons salt
- 3 tablespoons or 3 packages yeast
- 6 cups lukewarm water
- 1 cup oil
- 1½ to 2 jalapeño peppers
- 4 cups shredded cheddar cheese
- 10 eggs

INSTRUCTIONS:

1. In large bowl, mix 5 cups flour, sugar, salt, and yeast. Add water and oil. Beat well. Add 13 cups flour, mixing well as dough thickens.
2. Knead well then let rise in warm place until doubled, approximately 1 hour.
3. In blender, chop jalapeño peppers. Add cheese and eggs. Blend until well mixed.
4. Put egg mixture in large bowl. Pinch golf-ball-sized chunks of dough and pitch them into egg mixture. Mix dough into egg mixture until well blended.
5. Grease 8 loaf pans well, including upper edges.
6. Spoon batter into loaf pans, dividing evenly between them.
7. Let rise 30 to 45 minutes.
8. Bake at 350 degrees for 30 to 45 minutes.

Emma Gingerich, *Mt. Ayr, IA*

EASY FROSTED CINNAMON ROLLS

My mother-in-law used to make these rolls to sell in her baked-goods stand.

ROLLS INGREDIENTS:

- 1½ cups boiling water or milk
- 1 cup butter
- 2 tablespoons yeast
- ½ cup sugar
- 1 tablespoon salt
- ½ cup warm water
- 2 eggs, beaten
- 5 cups flour (approximately)
- 4 tablespoons butter, softened
- Cinnamon
- Brown sugar

FROSTING INGREDIENTS:

- 1 cup butter or margarine, softened
- 2 cups brown sugar
- ½ cup heavy cream
- 4 cups powdered sugar
- 2 teaspoons vanilla

ROLLS INSTRUCTIONS:

1. In bowl, pour boiling water over 1 cup butter, stirring to melt. Cool.
2. In another bowl, dissolve yeast, sugar, and salt in warm water.
3. Pour yeast mixture into butter mixture. Add eggs and mix well.
4. Add enough flour to form soft dough.
5. Roll dough out into ¼-inch thick rectangle and spread with 4 tablespoons butter. Sprinkle with cinnamon and brown sugar to taste.
6. Roll dough up from long side and cut ½-inch slices. Place in greased baking pans.
7. Let rise 1½ to 2 hours.
8. Bake at 350 degrees for 20 to 25 minutes.
9. Frost while warm.

Makes 4 small pans.

FROSTING INSTRUCTIONS:

Mix all ingredients together until smooth.

Lizzie Miller, *Bremen, OH*

OVERNIGHT CINNAMON ROLLS

INGREDIENTS:

¾ cup shortening
¾ cup sugar
2 eggs
2½ teaspoons salt
2⅓ cups warm water
2 tablespoons instant yeast
7½ cups flour
Butter, softened
Brown sugar
Cinnamon

INSTRUCTIONS:

1. In mixing bowl, cream shortening, sugar, eggs, and salt.
2. Add water, yeast, and flour. Knead well.
3. Place in bowl with cover and refrigerate for 8 hours or overnight.
4. Roll out dough and spread with butter, brown sugar, and cinnamon.
5. Cut in 1½-inch pieces. Let rise 1 hour on baking pan.
6. Bake at 325 degrees for 15 minutes or until golden brown.
7. Frost with a caramel frosting.

Jolene Bontrager, *Topeka, IN*

STRAWBERRY ROLLS

INGREDIENTS:

- 1½ tablespoons yeast
- ¼ cup lukewarm water
- ½ teaspoon sugar
- 1 stick margarine or butter, melted
- 1 cup milk
- ⅓ cup sugar
- 2 teaspoons salt
- 1 cup lukewarm water
- 6 cups flour
- 3 eggs
- 2 cups strawberry pie filling

INSTRUCTIONS:

1. In bowl, combine yeast, ¼ cup lukewarm water, and ½ teaspoon sugar; set aside.
2. In mixing bowl, combine melted margarine, milk, ⅓ cup sugar, and salt and blend well.
3. Add 1 cup lukewarm water then add yeast mixture. Mix well.
4. Add 3 cups flour. Mix well.
5. Beat eggs until frothy and add to mixture. Add 3 more cups flour. Mix well.
6. Let rise to double the size.
7. Unless you have plenty of counter space, work with half of the dough and roll out. Spread with 1 cup strawberry pie filling. If it looks like it's not enough filling, don't worry; it is. You don't want filling pouring out of rolls. Roll dough up from long side and slice 1-inch pieces. Place in greased pan.
8. Do the same to other half of dough.
9. Let rise to double size.
10. Bake at 350 degrees for 25 to 30 minutes until golden on top.
11. Top with your favorite icing recipe

Makes 4 (9 inch) pans.

Barbara Eicher, *Kentucky*

PUMPKIN CINNAMON ROLLS

INGREDIENTS:

2¼ cups milk
¾ cup sugar
1 teaspoon salt
1 cup pumpkin puree
½ cup butter
2 eggs
2 tablespoons yeast
5½ to 6 cups flour
¼ cup melted butter
¾ cup brown sugar
Cinnamon

INSTRUCTIONS:

1. In saucepan, heat milk to boiling. Remove from heat and add sugar, salt, pumpkin, and butter. Let cool to 120 degrees.
2. Add eggs and beat very well. Add yeast and 2 cups flour. Beat well again. Add remaining 3½ to 4 cups flour, mixing well.
3. Let rise in warm place for 1 hour.
4. Roll out to desired thickness. Spread with melted butter, brown sugar, and a good sprinkling of cinnamon. Roll up and slice into 1-inch slices. Place in greased aluminum pie pans.
5. Let rise for 30 minutes.
6. Bake at 400 degrees for 15 to 20 minutes.
7. Frost with your desired icing.

Ruby Ann Hochstettler, *New Holstein, WI*

MAPLE TWIST ROLLS

DOUGH INGREDIENTS:

¾ cup milk
¼ cup butter
1¾ cups bread flour
3 tablespoons sugar
½ teaspoon salt
1 tablespoon yeast
1 teaspoon maple flavoring
1 egg
1 cup doughnut mix
¼ cup melted butter

FILLING INGREDIENTS:

½ cup brown sugar
½ cup chopped nuts
1 teaspoon cinnamon
1 teaspoon maple flavoring

FROSTING INGREDIENTS:

9 tablespoons brown sugar
3 tablespoons butter, melted
6 tablespoons cream

DOUGH INSTRUCTIONS:

1. In saucepan, heat milk and butter until very warm.
2. In large mixer bowl, blend on low speed warm liquid with 1 cup flour, sugar, salt, yeast, maple flavoring, and egg. Blend until moistened then beat 2 minutes on medium speed.
3. By hand, mix in ¾ cup flour and doughnut mix to form soft dough.
4. Knead on floured surface until smooth and elastic.
5. Place dough in greased bowl. Cover and let rise until double in size.
6. Grease 3 (12 inch) pizza pans.
7. Divide dough into 3 balls. Roll 1 ball of dough to cover a pan. Brush with melted butter and sprinkle with filling. Repeat with other 2 balls of dough.
8. Use scissors to cut dough from outside circle to center to create wedges. Twist each wedge. Set on baking sheets and cover to rise.
9. Bake at 375 degrees for 18 to 22 minutes.
10. When cooled, frost.

FILLING INSTRUCTIONS:

Mix all ingredients together well.

FROSTING INSTRUCTIONS:

Combine ingredients and drizzle over top of baked rolls.

Lovina J. Gingerich, *Dalton, OH*

BAKED CREAM STICKS

DOUGH INGREDIENTS:

- 2 cups warm water
- 2 tablespoons yeast
- ¼ cup sugar
- 3 cups doughnut mix
- 2 cups bread flour
- 1 teaspoon salt

FILLING INGREDIENTS:

- 1 tube Bavarian pie filling
- 20 ounces whipped topping
- 12 ounces cream cheese, softened

CARAMEL ICING INGREDIENTS:

- ¾ cup butter
- 1½ cups brown sugar
- ¾ cup milk or evaporated milk
- 4 cups powdered sugar

DOUGH INSTRUCTIONS:

1. In bowl, mix water, yeast, and sugar. Let sit until bubbly.
2. Add doughnut mix, bread flour, and salt. Mix well. Let rise.
3. Use rolling pin to roll out large rectangle of dough ½-inch thick.
4. Use pizza cutter to cut dough into small or large rectangular pieces.
5. Set dough rectangles on greased pans and let rise 20 minutes.
6. Bake at 350 degrees for 15 minutes.
7. While still warm, use wooden spoon handle to poke hole through one end of cream stick.
8. When cool, fill with filling then ice.

FILLING INSTRUCTIONS:

1. In bowl, mix together pie filling, whipped topping, and cream cheese until smooth.
2. Fill pastry decorating bag and squeeze filling into hole placed in cream stick.

CARAMEL ICING INSTRUCTIONS:

1. In saucepan, melt butter with brown sugar.
2. Add milk and bring to boiling point.
3. Remove from heat; cool slightly. Add powdered sugar, stirring until smooth.
4. Cool until thickened but still easily spreadable.

Barbara Coblentz, *Greenfield, OH*
Mrs. Henry Gingerich, *Whitesville, NY*
Ada Miller, *Hillsboro, OH*

BANANA BREAD

INGREDIENTS:

- 1¼ cups sugar
- ½ cup margarine or butter
- 2 eggs, beaten
- 1½ cups mashed ripe banana
- ½ cup buttermilk
- 1 teaspoon vanilla
- 2½ cups flour
- 2 teaspoons baking powder
- ½ teaspoon salt
- ¼ teaspoon baking soda
- 1 cup chopped nuts

INSTRUCTIONS:

1. Preheat oven to 350 degrees.
2. In mixing bowl, blend sugar and margarine. Mix in eggs and banana. Add buttermilk and vanilla.
3. Stir in flour, baking powder, salt, and baking soda. Mix in nuts.
4. Grease only the bottom of 2 loaf pans.
5. Divide batter into pans and bake for 1 hour.

Martha Beachy, *Butler, OH*

FAVORITE ZUCCHINI BREAD

INGREDIENTS:

- 3 eggs
- 1½ cups sugar
- 1 cup vegetable oil
- 2 teaspoons vanilla
- 3 cups flour
- 1 teaspoon baking soda
- 1 teaspoon baking powder
- 1 teaspoon salt
- 1 teaspoon cinnamon
- 2 cups shredded zucchini
- ½ cup chopped nuts

INSTRUCTIONS:

1. Preheat oven to 325 degrees.
2. In large bowl, combine eggs and sugar. Beat in oil and vanilla.
3. In another bowl, combine flour, baking soda, baking powder, salt, and cinnamon. Gradually add to sugar mixture and mix well. Stir in zucchini and nuts.
4. Divide into 2 greased 5x9-inch loaf pans.
5. Bake for 55 to 60 minutes or until toothpick inserted near center comes out clean.
6. Cool for 10 minutes before removing from pans and placing on wire cooling rack.
7. Delicious warm with butter.

Lori Miller, *Middlefield, OH*

SOFT PRETZELS

INGREDIENTS:

1 rounded tablespoon yeast
2 scant cups warm water
4 cups flour
1 cup pastry flour
½ cup brown sugar
¾ cup powdered sugar
2 teaspoons salt
1 tablespoon oil
4 teaspoons baking soda
1 cup warm water
Butter, melted
Coarse salt

INSTRUCTIONS:

1. Preheat oven to 450 degrees.
2. In bowl, dissolve yeast in 2 scant cups warm water. Set aside.
3. In mixing bowl, mix flour, pastry flour, brown sugar, powdered sugar, and salt. Add yeast mixture and oil, mixing well to form dough.
4. Flatten dough onto cutting board. Use pizza cutter to cut strips of dough. Roll and shape. The less you work the dough, the softer the pretzel will be.
5. In bowl, mix baking soda in 1 cup warm water.
6. Dip shaped dough into soda water. Set on baking sheets and let rise just a little.
7. Bake 8 to 10 minutes.
8. Dip pretzels into melted butter then sprinkle with salt.
9. Serve with cheese sauce. Or sprinkle with cinnamon and sugar for a sweet treat.

Fannie Ann Byler, *Reynoldsville, PA*

THE ALMOST-AMISH RECIPES I WAS RAISED ON

I may not be Amish, but I sure like eating as if I were! And I realized that many of my favorite foods, passed down through generations of my family, are the same foods enjoyed by Amish families today.

I decided to share my family recipes for a typical meal consisting of meat, a couple of sides, and a dessert. And each recipe would be quick and easy to prepare, making it both delicious and accessible to modern cooks without a lot of time.

Raising a big family of six hungry kids, my parents were good at providing well-balanced meals that combined protein, carbs, and fat—oh, and veggies! Somehow, they were always delicious too—except on hash night. I never could stand hash, especially corn beef hash.

When I was raising my own five children, I found myself turning often to the time-tested recipes my parents had often prepared—recipes passed down to them by their own parents and grandparents. I come from a blended heritage of Irish, Dutch, and German, so you can imagine the richness of potential meals my parents had to pull from!

We ate things like Irish stew with homemade dumplings; wonderfully moist homemade meat loaf; ham, cabbage, and potatoes; potato pancakes; pot roast with all the fixings; spaghetti with homemade sauce; bratwurst and huge meatballs; and so much more! Many of these things are Old World foods enjoyed by immigrants from Europe. They brought with them the recipes and foods that they'd grown up with, and that gave them the comfort of a taste of home in a new land. Many Amish cooks have descended from similar ancestral lines and cook similar recipes in their kitchens today!

Like my busy parents, I enjoy homemade food but don't necessarily have the time to prepare it the way those long-ago relatives did. . .or the way Amish cooks spend hours in their kitchens today preparing scrumptious dishes for their loved ones. So I've incorporated little shortcuts that make these recipes practical for today's busy cook who wants to serve traditional, wholesome meals to her family but often needs to do so after getting home from a full day's work outside the home. She may not have time or space for a garden either, so it's fine to use canned or frozen fruits and veggies instead of fresh if you don't have any. They're also more affordable.

At the end of the day, do as I've done: Take these recipes and make them your own! Experiment. Substitute. Add and subtract. And soon you'll be creating your own culinary traditions to pass down to your children.

Enjoy!

Anne Blackburne

Anne lives and works in Southeast Ohio as a newspaper editor and writer of Amish fiction. She has five grown children and a spoiled poodle named Millie.

NOURISHING *the* FAMILY

And they, continuing daily with one accord in the temple, and breaking bread from house to house, did eat their meat with gladness and singleness of heart.

~ Acts 2:46

WEDDING CHICKEN SEASONING

Most Amish weddings consist of a few basic dishes: butter noodles, mashed potatoes, coleslaw, yeast rolls or fresh bread, and chicken. I've eaten chicken made in various ways, but my favorite was at the wedding of young Anna Mary and Paul, where the chicken had been grilled all morning with a special blend of seasonings then stored in coolers, where it continued to cook in its own heat until served. Instead of baked chicken and stuffing dishes common to Pennsylvania, grilling is a favorite of our communities here in northern Kentucky.

INGREDIENTS:

Lemon pepper
Garlic powder
Seasoning salt

INSTRUCTIONS:

1. Fill shaker with equal parts of all ingredients.
2. Sprinkle seasoning on chicken a few times while grilling.

Mindy Steele, *Kentucky*

SUMMER SALAD MEAL

INGREDIENTS:

1 pound ground beef
1 small onion, chopped
1 (16 ounce) can pork & beans
Lettuce
Potatoes, cooked and diced
Eggs, hard-boiled and sliced
Radishes, sliced
Carrots, shredded
Tomatoes, diced
Celery, chopped
Cheese, shredded

INSTRUCTIONS:

1. In large skillet, fry beef and onion together until done. Add pork & beans and heat to boiling. Remove from heat.
2. On large platter, layer lettuce, potatoes, eggs, radishes, carrots, tomatoes, and celery in amounts to accommodate your family. Pour beef and bean mixture over top and sprinkle with cheese.
3. Serve with cheese sauce or your favorite dressing.

Edna Miller, *Nashville, MI*

HAM AND CHEESE STICKY BUNS

INGREDIENTS:

1 cup butter
⅓ cup brown sugar
2 tablespoons mustard
2 tablespoons poppy seeds
2 tablespoons Worcestershire sauce
24 dinner rolls
Ham, thinly sliced
Swiss cheese or other cheese of preference

INSTRUCTIONS:

1. Preheat oven to 350 degrees.
2. In saucepan, combine butter, brown sugar, mustard, poppy seeds, and Worcestershire sauce and heat until melted together.
3. Cut rolls in half. Fill with ham and cheese. Set each little sandwich in 9x13-inch cake pan touching each other.
4. Pour sauce over top.
5. Cover with foil and bake 20 minutes.

Lizzie Hostetler, *Polk, OH*

BIEROCKS

DOUGH INGREDIENTS:

- 1 tablespoon sugar
- 1 tablespoon yeast
- 1 cup warm water
- 3 eggs, beaten
- ½ cup sugar
- 1 teaspoon salt
- ½ cup melted butter
- 5 cups flour

FILLING INGREDIENTS:

- 1 pound ground beef
- 1 tablespoon taco seasoning
- 1 tablespoon chopped onion
- 1 cup pizza sauce
- 1 cup shredded cheese

DOUGH INSTRUCTIONS:

1. In bowl, mix 1 tablespoon sugar, yeast, and warm water. Let stand 5 minutes.
2. Add eggs, ½ cup sugar, salt, and melted butter. Mix well.
3. Stir in flour to form dough and knead.
4. Let rise until doubled.
5. Prepare filling.
6. Roll dough out and cut into approximately 5-inch squares.
7. Place about 2 tablespoons filling in middle of square. Fold corners up and pinch together.
8. Place buns fold side down on parchment-lined pans without touching each other. Let rise a little.
9. Bake at 350 degrees for 25 to 30 minutes or until brown.
10. You can brush tops with melted butter before serving.

FILLING INSTRUCTIONS:

1. In skillet, brown beef. Add taco seasoning and onion. Mix in pizza sauce.
2. Remove from heat and stir in cheese.
3. Keep warm until ready to fill dough.

Mrs. Edward Yoder, *Burke, NY*

SAUCY BARBECUED MEATBALLS

MEATBALL INGREDIENTS:

- 3 pounds ground beef
- 2 cups oatmeal or crushed saltines
- 2 cups milk
- 2 eggs, beaten
- 1 large onion, chopped
- 2 teaspoons salt
- ½ teaspoon pepper
- 2 teaspoons chili powder

SAUCE INGREDIENTS:

- 2 cups ketchup
- 2 cups water
- 3 cups brown sugar
- 4 tablespoons liquid smoke
- 1 teaspoon garlic powder

MEATBALL INSTRUCTIONS:

Mix all ingredients together and form 1-inch meatballs. Place in baking dish.

SAUCE INSTRUCTIONS:

1. Mix all ingredients together and pour over meatballs.
2. Bake at 350 degrees for 1 hour.

Mrs. Andy (Malinda) Gingerich, *Hartford, KS*

PULLED PORK

INGREDIENTS:

- 4 tablespoons mustard
- 1 (7 to 8 pound) pork shoulder roast
- 1½ tablespoons salt
- ½ teaspoon garlic powder
- 1½ teaspoons pepper
- 2 tablespoons paprika
- 1 tablespoon chili powder
- Barbecue sauce

INSTRUCTIONS:

1. Preheat oven to 325 degrees.
2. Spread mustard over roast.
3. In bowl, combine salt, garlic powder, pepper, paprika, and chili powder and rub into roast.
4. Place roast in roasting pan. Cover tightly and bake for 16 hours.
5. Pull roast with forks and mix with barbecue sauce.

Linda Fisher, *Ronks, PA*

SAUSAGE ROLLS

INGREDIENTS:

- 2 pounds prepared cinnamon roll dough
- 2 eggs, beaten
- 3 teaspoons dried parsley
- 1 teaspoon onion powder
- 1 teaspoon garlic powder
- ½ teaspoon oregano
- 1 pound smoked sausage, thinly sliced or diced
- 1 pound shredded cheese

INSTRUCTIONS:

1. Preheat oven to 350 degrees.
2. Roll dough out into large rectangle around ¼-inch thick.
3. In bowl, mix eggs, parsley, onion powder, garlic powder, and oregano. Stir in sausage.
4. Spread mixture over dough and top with cheese.
5. Roll up dough from long side and cut into ½-inch slices. Place on baking sheet lined with parchment paper.
6. Bake for 45 minutes.

Eli and Elsie Miller, *Thurman, OH*

CHICKEN POTPIE

PASTRY INGREDIENTS:

- 2⅓ cups flour
- 1½ teaspoons celery seed
- ⅔ cup cold butter, grated
- 2 (8 ounce) packages cream cheese, softened

GRAVY INGREDIENTS:

- ⅓ cup butter
- ⅓ cup flour
- 1 tablespoon minced garlic
- 1½ cups chicken broth
- 1½ cups milk
- 1 teaspoon salt
- 1 teaspoon Better Than Bouillon chicken flavoring
- ½ to 1 teaspoon pepper
- ¾ cup diced potatoes
- 1½ cups frozen mixed vegetables
- 2 cups cubed cooked chicken

PASTRY INSTRUCTIONS:

1. In bowl, combine flour and celery seed. Cut in butter and cream cheese.
2. Work dough by hand until it forms ball.
3. On lightly floured surface, roll out dough, cutting into 4 (10 inch) circles.
4. Line 2 pie plates with dough circles. Set aside remaining 2 circles.

GRAVY INSTRUCTIONS:

1. Preheat oven to 425 degrees.
2. In heavy saucepan, melt butter. Add flour and garlic. Gradually add broth and milk.
3. Bring to boil and cook for 2 minutes.
4. Remove from heat and add salt, chicken flavoring, and pepper.
5. In separate kettle, cover potatoes and mixed vegetables with water and bring to boil, cooking until just tender. Drain.
6. Add vegetables and chicken to gravy, mixing well.
7. Pour gravy mixture into crust-lined pie pans.
8. Use remaining dough to top pies. Cut vents. (This is optional and can be skipped if you prefer no top crust.)
9. Bake for 30 minutes until crust is golden.

Brenda Graber, *Hamptonville, NC*

CRISPY FRIED FISH

INGREDIENTS:

½ cup cornmeal
½ cup flour
1 cup crushed
cracker crumbs
½ teaspoon baking powder
1 teaspoon sugar
1 teaspoon salt
¼ teaspoon pepper
2 pounds fish fillets
Milk

INSTRUCTIONS:

1. In bowl, mix cornmeal, flour, cracker crumbs, baking powder, sugar, salt, and pepper.
2. Dip fish in milk or water.
3. Drop fish in crumb mixture and coat.
4. Fry in deep hot oil until browned on both sides.

Mrs. Sarah Petersheim, *Diagonal, IA*

NO-LEFTOVERS HOMEMADE MEAT LOAF

A family favorite when I was growing up was my dad's homemade meat loaf. Unlike some of the very fine-grained meat loaves I've seen, Dad's recipe is chunky with pieces of bread, onions, and ground beef. It's also very moist, and there are almost never any leftovers—which is sad, because I do love a good meat loaf sandwich!

You'll need a big mixing bowl and a baking pan. I've tried different pans, from bread loaf pans to big 11x13 baking dishes. It all works, although cooking time may vary depending on the thickness of the loaf.

INGREDIENTS:

2 pounds ground beef

¼ cup chopped onion, fresh or frozen; or 2 tablespoons dehydrated onion

2 slices bread

2 large eggs

½ cup milk

½ cup ketchup

Salt and pepper to taste

INSTRUCTIONS:

1. Preheat oven to 350 degrees.
2. Plop ground beef and onion into big bowl.
3. Tear bread into smallish, not tiny, pieces and toss them in.
4. Crack eggs into bowl and add milk. Add ketchup, and toss in salt and pepper to taste.
5. Then get your (clean) hands in there and start mixing it all up. It's going to be cold since the hamburger just came out of the fridge. Squish it all up into a nice mixture, and then form it into loaf shape in baking dish.
6. Bake uncovered about 1 hour. It'll be nicely browned on top, and the meat will be cooked through if you cut into it, not pink. Any juices should be clear, and a meat thermometer should register 160 degrees.

NOTES:

- This recipe can be doubled.
- To feed my family of seven when I was raising my kids, I'd use two pounds of ground beef. I don't use the ultra-lean beef recommended in some recipes, because I might want to make gravy.
- You can substitute many of the ingredients as you like. Sometimes my family gets adventurous, and we'll use barbecue sauce instead of ketchup.
- You can add other veggies if you like. I always thought it would be a great way to hide peas, but my kids were too clever for me and rejected that. Oh, well!
- The Amish like to do this old favorite a bit differently, by making a ketchup glaze to put on top. They may also put strips of bacon on top, under the glaze. They sometimes use oats or quick oats rather than bread, to make it gluten-free.
- I've occasionally substituted Stovetop stuffing for the bread (one 6-ounce box), and it's delicious! You can use crumbled crackers too (a sleeve of crushed crackers). This is a very versatile recipe. The key is to use plenty of ketchup or barbecue sauce, and don't forget that half cup of milk to ensure moisture.
- It's great served with mashed potatoes and gravy you can make with the pan drippings. Or try it with brown-buttered noodles and stewed tomatoes as sides! Delicious hot as a meal and cold in sandwiches—if there are any leftovers! Enjoy!

Anne Blackburne, *Ohio*

SALISBURY STEAK

INGREDIENTS:

1 pound ground beef
¾ cup fine cracker crumbs
1 tablespoon minced onion
½ teaspoon salt
½ teaspoon pepper
½ cup tomato sauce
2 eggs
2 cups brown gravy

INSTRUCTIONS:

1. Preheat oven to 350 degrees.
2. In bowl, combine ground beef, cracker crumbs, onion, salt, pepper, tomato sauce, and eggs. Mix well. Form into oblong patties using about ½ cup mixture each.
3. In skillet, brown on both sides in oil.
4. Place in casserole dish, then pour gravy over patties.
5. Cover and bake for 1 hour.

Mrs. Menno Miller, *Gallipolis, OH*

CREAMY POTATO TOPPING

INGREDIENTS:

1 pound ground beef
½ cup finely chopped onion
2 tablespoons lard or butter
6 tablespoons flour
1 teaspoon salt
⅛ teaspoon pepper
3½ cups milk
½ cup shredded cheese or cream cheese
2 cups cooked, drained peas (optional)
Baked or mashed potatoes

INSTRUCTIONS:

1. In skillet, brown beef and onion in lard. Mix in flour, salt, and pepper. Stir in milk, cooking and stirring constantly until mixture boils and thickens.
2. Reduce heat to low. Add cheese, stirring until melted. Gently stir in peas.
3. Serve over potatoes.

Janet Weaver, *Lititz, PA*

CHICKEN-N-STUFFING CASSEROLE

CASSEROLE INGREDIENTS:

- 6 cups breadcrumbs, toasted
- ¼ cup diced celery
- 1 tablespoon chopped onion
- 1 tablespoon parsley flakes
- 2 eggs
- ¼ cup butter
- Salt and pepper to taste

TOPPING INGREDIENTS:

- ¼ cup butter
- 4 tablespoons flour
- 1 cup chicken broth
- 1 can cream of chicken soup
- 1 can milk (use soup can to measure)
- 1 whole chicken, cooked and cut up (or use canned chicken)
- Salt and pepper to taste

CASSEROLE INSTRUCTIONS:

1. Mix all ingredients and add hot water to moisten.
2. Place in greased 9x13-inch baking pan.

TOPPING INSTRUCTIONS:

1. Preheat oven to 375 degrees.
2. In saucepan, melt butter and thicken with flour to form paste. Add broth, soup, and milk. Cook until thick gravy forms.
3. Add chicken and season with salt and pepper to taste.
4. Pour over breadcrumb mixture.
5. Bake for 1 hour.

Betty H. Byler, *Smicksburg, PA*

ROOSTER CASSEROLE

I once visited an Amish friend who was in the process of preparing supper, and I asked her what she was preparing. Her family raised not only horses but a large flock of chickens. She told me Rooster Casserole and smiled wildly. This dish actually inspired my character Hannah in Cicada Season. *I still laugh every time I make this dish, knowing she is one ornery rooster short now.*

INGREDIENTS:

- ½ cup chopped onion
- ½ cup chopped celery
- 2 cloves garlic, minced
- ½ cup butter
- ½ cup flour
- 2 teaspoons sugar
- 1 teaspoon salt
- 1 teaspoon pepper
- 4 cups chicken broth
- 1 can peas and carrots, or 1 (10 ounce) bag frozen peas and carrots
- 4 cups cooked and cubed pesky rooster or chicken
- 1 small bowl of your favorite biscuit dough or 1 can biscuit dough

INSTRUCTIONS:

1. Preheat oven to 350 degrees.
2. In large saucepan, sauté onion, celery, and garlic in butter. Add flour, sugar, salt, pepper, and broth. Bring to boil and stir constantly as it thickens.
3. Reduce heat and add peas and carrots and cooked rooster. Heat through.
4. Pour into baking dish and drop dough on top.
5. Bake for 30 minutes until biscuit dough is completely done.

Mindy Steele, *Kentucky*

HAMBURGER NOODLE CASSEROLE

INGREDIENTS:

2 pounds ground beef
2 medium onions, chopped
10 ounces noodles
1 large jar Cheese Whiz or 12 ounces Velveeta cheese
2 cans cream of mushroom soup
Salt and pepper to taste
Shredded cheese

INSTRUCTIONS:

1. Preheat oven to 350 degrees.
2. In skillet, fry beef and onions until done; drain.
3. In pot, cook noodles according to package directions; drain.
4. Add noodles, cheese, and soup to hamburger. Season to taste with salt and pepper. Mix well.
5. Place in casserole dish. Top with shredded cheese.
6. Bake for 30 to 40 minutes until hot and bubbly.

Malinda Gingerich, *Spartansburg, PA*

RICE AND CHICKEN CASSEROLE

INGREDIENTS:

1 cup white rice
1 cup chopped celery
¾ cup chopped onion
2 teaspoons parsley
½ teaspoon salt
¼ teaspoon pepper
1 can cream of mushroom soup
¾ cup mayonnaise
2 cups chicken broth
2 cups cooked, chopped chicken

INSTRUCTIONS:

1. Preheat oven to 350 degrees.
2. Mix all ingredients together and place in baking dish.
3. Cover and bake for 1½ hours.
4. It is a very forgiving recipe. Add your own favorites. I like to add cooked potatoes and carrots or substitute rice with raw potatoes and carrots with cook time adjusted to 2½ hours.

Katie Beiler, *Christiana, PA*

Pioneer

CHICKEN BACON RANCH CASSEROLE

INGREDIENTS:

1 (16 ounce) package spiral pasta
1½ cups milk
½ cup ranch salad dressing
1 envelope ranch salad dressing mix
1 (8 ounce) package cream cheese, cubed
2 cups cooked, cubed chicken
8 strips bacon, cooked and crumbled
2 cups shredded Colby cheese
Green onions, sliced (optional)

INSTRUCTIONS:

1. Preheat oven to 400 degrees.
2. In large saucepan, cook pasta according to package directions. Drain and place in large bowl.
3. In same saucepan, combine milk, salad dressing, and dressing mix until smooth. Stir in cream cheese, and cook over medium heat, stirring until melted. Pour over pasta and stir to coat.
4. Mix in chicken, bacon, and 1 cup cheese. Transfer to greased 9x13-inch baking dish. Top with remaining 1 cup cheese.
5. Bake for 15 to 20 minutes until heated through and cheese is melted.
6. Sprinkle with green onions before serving if desired.

Lucinda Eicher, *Monroe, IN*

DANDELION GRAVY

INGREDIENTS:

½ cup bacon grease
1 cup flour
6 cups milk
2 to 3 teaspoons apple cider vinegar
1 teaspoon salt
Pepper to taste
½ cup brown sugar (optional)
3 tablespoons sugar (optional)
Boiled eggs, sliced
Dandelion greens, chopped
Bacon, cooked and crumbled

INSTRUCTIONS:

1. In skillet, melt bacon grease. Add flour and brown lightly. Stir in milk; keep stirring until thickened.
2. Add vinegar, salt, pepper, brown sugar, and sugar. (Sugars can be omitted, but they bring out more of the flavor.) Heat through but do not boil.
3. Add eggs, greens, and bacon.
4. Very good served over biscuits or mashed potatoes.

Note: Greens are best cut in early March to April. But you can also eat the gravy without the greens.

Mrs. Anna Raber, *Millersburg, OH*

BUBBLE AND SQUEAK

INGREDIENTS:

1 pound bulk sausage
1 onion, diced
4 to 6 medium potatoes, sliced
½ head cabbage, chopped
⅓ cup apple cider vinegar
Cheese

INSTRUCTIONS:

1. In deep skillet, sauté sausage and onion.
2. Add potatoes and fry over low heat until potatoes are halfway done.
3. Add cabbage and fry until almost soft.
4. Stir in vinegar and cook a few minutes to blend flavors.
5. Melt some cheese on top before serving.

Katie Gingerich, *Dalton, OH*

WALNUT CREEK
150
TWP.

GARDEN FRESH STIR-FRY

INGREDIENTS:

- 6 tablespoons butter
- 1 cup sliced carrots
- 2 cups chunked (1 inch) potatoes
- 1 cup fresh cut green beans
- ½ cup diced onion
- ½ cup water
- 1½ cups broccoli florets
- 1½ cups cauliflower florets
- 1½ cups diced zucchini or summer squash
- 1 cup peas
- ½ cup chopped green pepper
- Seasoned salt
- 1½ pounds bulk sausage
- 2 tablespoons butter
- 2 tablespoons flour
- ½ teaspoon pepper
- 2½ cups milk

INSTRUCTIONS:

1. In large heavy skillet, melt 6 tablespoons butter over bottom. Layer carrots, potatoes, green beans, and onion. Add water. Cover and simmer 5 minutes.
2. Add broccoli, cauliflower, zucchini, peas, and green pepper. Season to taste with seasoned salt. Cover and simmer.
3. In another skillet, brown sausage. Add 2 tablespoons butter, flour, and pepper, mixing into sausage.
4. Turn heat to low and slowly add milk, stirring with whisk. Heat to boiling.
5. Pour over cooked vegetables.

Mrs. Susie Byler, *Brockway, PA*

HOMEMADE SHAKE 'N' BAKE

INGREDIENTS:

- 4 cups flour
- 4 cups fine cracker crumbs
- 2 tablespoons salt
- 1 tablespoon sugar
- 3 tablespoons paprika
- 2 teaspoons pepper
- ½ cup cooking oil

INSTRUCTIONS:

1. Preheat oven to 350 degrees.
2. Mix all ingredients together.
3. Salt chicken pieces then coat with mixture. Place on greased cookie sheets.
4. Bake for 45 minutes (depending on size of pieces). Cover with foil and continue baking if chicken is not yet tender. Internal temperature of chicken should reach 170 degrees.

Mrs. Ura Gingerich, *Wellsville, NY*

HUSBAND'S DELIGHT

INGREDIENTS:

- 1 (8 ounce) package cream cheese, softened
- 2 cups sour cream or 1 cup milk
- 1 small onion, chopped
- 1½ pounds ground beef
- 2 tablespoons butter
- 16 ounces pizza sauce
- ½ teaspoon Worcestershire sauce
- Salt and pepper to taste
- 10 ounces noodles
- Velveeta cheese

INSTRUCTIONS:

1. Preheat oven to 350 degrees.
2. In bowl, blend cream cheese, sour cream, and onion.
3. In skillet, brown beef in butter. Add pizza sauce and Worcestershire sauce. Season with salt and pepper to taste.
4. In saucepan, cook noodles according to package directions to tenderness preference.
5. In 2-quart saucepan, layer cooked noodles, beef mixture, and cream cheese mixture. Top with slices of Velveeta cheese.
6. Bake for 30 to 45 minutes until heated through and bubbly.

Ella A. Hershberger, *Sullivan, OH*

WARM GARDEN VEGGIE PIZZA

We make this pizza throughout the summer, using our fresh garden vegetables. My little brother isn't too fond of vegetables, but he likes this pizza. Dip slices in ranch dressing or barbecue sauce. Delicious! Really good served with watermelon.

PIZZA INGREDIENTS:

- Your favorite pizza dough (or see below)
- 3 tablespoons olive oil
- ½ teaspoon garlic salt
- 1 teaspoon oregano
- 1 teaspoon parsley
- Pepper slices
- Onion slices
- Tomato, diced
- Cucumber slices
- Zucchini slices
- Cabbage, diced
- Spinach
- Mozzarella cheese, shredded

CRUST INGREDIENTS:

- 1 cup warm water
- 1 tablespoon yeast
- 2 tablespoons sugar
- 2 tablespoons oil
- 1 teaspoon salt
- 2½ cups flour

PIZZA INSTRUCTIONS:

1. Preheat oven to 350 degrees.
2. Spread dough onto pizza pan.
3. In bowl, mix olive oil, garlic salt, oregano, and parsley. Brush over dough.
4. Bake for 20 minutes.
5. Remove from oven and top with vegetables of your choice and cover with cheese.
6. Bake 15 more minutes or until toppings are crisp and hot.

Anna Swartzentruber, *West Salem, OH*

CRUST INSTRUCTIONS:

1. In bowl, mix warm water and yeast. Add sugar. Let stand for 10 minutes.
2. Add oil, salt, and flour, mixing well.
3. Press into 2 round pizza pans.

Mary Gingerich, *Dalton, OH*

HAMBURGER TATER TOT CASSEROLE

A quick and easy dinner casserole.

INGREDIENTS:

2 pounds ground beef, browned

1 quart green beans, cooked and drained

1 can cream of mushroom soup

Cheese, shredded or sliced

Bacon, cooked and crumbled

1 bag tater tots

INSTRUCTIONS:

1. Preheat oven to 350 degrees.
2. In bowl, mix beef, green beans, and soup.
3. Spread into 9x13-inch casserole dish.
4. Top with your desired amount of cheese and bacon.
5. Arrange tater tots in single layer over all.
6. Bake uncovered for 1 hour.

Miriam Miller, *Hillsboro, OH*

SEVEN-LAYER SUPPER

This is a down-to-earth, healthy casserole.

INGREDIENTS:

- ½ pound bacon, chopped into 1-inch pieces, uncooked
- 1½ pounds ground beef, browned
- 4 potatoes, peeled and thinly sliced
- 1 onion, sliced
- 4 carrots, thinly sliced
- ½ teaspoon salt
- ½ to 1 teaspoon pepper
- ½ to 1 teaspoon garlic salt
- ½ to 1 teaspoon seasoned salt
- 1 to 1½ cups water
- Cheese, shredded (optional)

INSTRUCTIONS:

1. Preheat oven to 350 degrees.
2. In 9x13-inch baking pan, layer in order bacon, beef, potatoes, onion, carrots, salt, pepper, garlic salt, and seasoned salt. Pour water over all until nearly covered.
3. Bake for 1½ hours. Top with cheese when nearly done.

Carolyn Lambright, *Lagrange, IN*

POTATO PATCH CASSEROLE

MEATBALL INGREDIENTS:

- 1 pound ground beef
- ½ cup chopped onion
- 1 egg
- ¼ cup milk
- ¼ cup breadcrumbs
- 1 teaspoon salt
- ¼ teaspoon celery salt
- Flour

WHITE SAUCE INGREDIENTS:

- 2 tablespoons butter
- 2 tablespoons flour
- 1⅓ cups milk
- 1¼ teaspoons salt
- ½ pound Velveeta cheese, cubed

VEGETABLE INGREDIENTS:

- 4 cups cooked, sliced potatoes
- 10 ounces sliced carrots

MEATBALL INSTRUCTIONS:

1. In bowl, combine beef, onion, egg, milk, breadcrumbs, salt, and celery salt. Shape into balls.
2. Roll in flour and brown in greased skillet. Set aside.

WHITE SAUCE INSTRUCTIONS:

1. In saucepan, melt butter and brown flour in it. Slowly stir in milk and stir until thickened.
2. Add salt and cubed cheese, stirring until cheese melts smoothly.

VEGETABLE INSTRUCTIONS:

1. Preheat oven to 350 degrees.
2. Place potatoes and carrots in casserole dish.
3. Layer meatballs on top.
4. Cover with white sauce.
5. Cover dish and bake for 1 hour.

Katie Esh, *Charlotte Court House, VA*

ZUCCHINI CASSEROLE

INGREDIENTS:

- 1 pound bulk sausage
- 5 cups shredded zucchini
- 3 eggs
- 1½ cups cracker crumbs
- ⅓ cup melted butter
- ½ teaspoon salt
- 2 cups shredded sharp cheese

INSTRUCTIONS:

1. Preheat oven to 350 degrees.
2. In skillet, fry sausage until no longer pink.
3. Add zucchini, eggs, cracker crumbs, butter, salt, and cheese. Place in casserole dish.
4. Cover and bake for 30 to 40 minutes until set and golden.

Anna M. Weaver, *Mertztown, PA*

ZUCCHINI SQUARES

INGREDIENTS:

- 3 cups shredded zucchini
- 4 eggs, beaten
- 1 cup Bisquick baking mix
- 1 cup Parmesan cheese
- ½ cup chopped onion
- ½ cup chopped green pepper
- ½ cup vegetable oil
- ½ teaspoon salt
- ½ teaspoon oregano
- ⅛ teaspoon garlic powder
- 2 teaspoons parsley flakes
- 1 cup sliced pepperoni
- ½ cup mozzarella cheese

INSTRUCTIONS:

1. Preheat oven to 350 degrees.
2. In bowl, mix zucchini, eggs, baking mix, Parmesan cheese, onion, green pepper, and oil. Season with salt, oregano, garlic powder, and parsley flakes. Fold in pepperoni.
3. Pour into 9x13 baking pan.
4. Bake 30 to 35 minutes.
5. Halfway through baking, sprinkle with mozzarella cheese.
6. It is done when knife inserted in center comes out clean.

Fannie Ann Byler, *Reynoldsville, PA*

TACO SALAD PIZZA

CRUST INGREDIENTS:

2 cups flour
2 teaspoons sugar
½ teaspoon salt
⅔ cup milk
4 teaspoons baking powder
½ teaspoon cream of tartar
½ cup shortening

CREAM LAYER INGREDIENTS:

2 cups sour cream
1 (8 ounce) package cream cheese, softened

TOPPING INGREDIENTS:

1½ pounds ground beef
1 envelope taco seasoning
1 pint pizza sauce
Cheese, shredded
Lettuce, shredded
Tomatoes, chopped
Tortilla chips, crushed

CRUST INSTRUCTIONS:

1. Preheat oven to 350 degrees.
2. Combine all ingredients, mixing well.
3. Press into 11x17-inch pan.
4. Bake for 15 minutes.

CREAM LAYER INSTRUCTIONS:

1. In bowl, beat together sour cream and cream cheese until smooth.
2. Spread on cooled crust.

TOPPING INSTRUCTIONS:

1. In skillet, brown beef then mix in taco seasoning and pizza sauce. Cool.
2. Spread cooled beef mixture over cream layer on crust. Top with shredded cheese.
3. Slice and serve with lettuce, tomatoes, and crushed chips.

Lizzie Shetler, *West Salem, OH*

HOAGIE PIZZA

INGREDIENTS:

- 1 cup warm water
- 2 tablespoons oil
- 1 teaspoon sugar
- 1 tablespoon yeast
- ½ teaspoon salt
- 2 cups flour
- Dash fresh or dried herbs (optional)
- ½ cup mayonnaise
- Mustard
- Chipped ham or meat of choice
- 1½ to 2 cups shredded cheese
- Thinly sliced vegetables of choice (lettuce, tomatoes, broccoli, onions, peppers, cucumbers)
- Italian dressing (optional)

INSTRUCTIONS:

1. Preheat oven to 375 degrees.
2. In bowl, combine warm water, oil, sugar, yeast, salt, flour, and herbs. Let sit for 10 minutes.
3. Dough will be sticky. Spread on pizza pan and let rise 10 minutes.
4. Bake for 30 to 40 minutes until lightly browned. Cool completely.
5. Spread with mayonnaise and mustard.
6. Top with ham and cheese.
7. Cover with vegetables of choice.
8. Drizzle with Italian dressing.

Simon and Tillie Yoder, *Hillsboro, WV*

ORGANIC
Peppers
Summer
Squash
Local
Eggplant
Local
CABBAGE
$2.50
head
RAINBOW
Heirloom
Tomatoes
50¢
SPECIAL
ORGANIC
CANNING
TOMATOES
$8.00
1/2 bu.
LOCAL
WATERMELONS
CANTALOPES
LOCALLY GROWN
1/2 BUSHEL
PRODUCE OF U.S.A.

POTATO PIZZA BAKE

INGREDIENTS:

- 1 pound ground beef
- 1 medium onion, chopped
- Salt and pepper to taste
- 4 cups thinly sliced potatoes
- 1 can cream of chicken soup
- ½ cup milk
- 1 pint pizza sauce
- Butter
- Velveeta cheese

INSTRUCTIONS:

1. Preheat oven to 375 degrees.
2. In skillet, lightly brown beef with onion. Salt and pepper to taste.
3. Line 9x13-inch casserole dish with potatoes. Top with meat.
4. In bowl, blend soup and milk. Pour over meat.
5. Pour pizza sauce over all and do not stir in.
6. Dot top with butter.
7. Bake covered for 1 hour.
8. Top with slices of cheese. Return to oven uncovered until melted.

Eli and Elsie Miller, *Thurman, OH*

TASTY SUPPER LOAF

INGREDIENTS:

Dough for 1 pizza crust

1 can cream of mushroom soup or mayonnaise

Shredded cheese

Bacon or sausage, fried and crumbled

Fried potatoes

Butter

INSTRUCTIONS:

1. Preheat oven to 375 to 400 degrees.
2. Divide dough in half. Roll half into rectangle on sheet of waxed paper.
3. Spread soup over dough within 1 inch from edges. Top with layer each of cheese, bacon, and potatoes. Add other toppings if desired.
4. Fold ends of dough then sides until all filling is hidden inside. Carefully pick up edges of waxed paper and quickly flip upside down onto greased cookie sheet. Cut small slits crosswise over dough to vent steam.
5. Repeat process with other half of dough.
6. Bake immediately for 15 minutes.
7. Brush with butter and desired seasonings.

Katie Byler, *Sugargrove, PA*

SCHMUCKER STEW

INGREDIENTS:

- 4 to 6 potatoes
- 1 pint carrots (optional)
- 2 pounds ground beef
- 2 quarts green beans, drained
- 1 can cream of mushroom soup
- 1½ pounds Velveeta cheese
- Salt and pepper to taste

INSTRUCTIONS:

1. In kettle, cook potatoes and carrots in a little water until soft.
2. In skillet, brown beef.
3. To kettle, add browned beef, green beans, soup, and cheese. Season with salt and pepper. Stir until cheese is melted and all is heated through.
4. For an even quicker meal, use all canned ingredients.

Sharon Rose Schmucker, *Mayslick, KY*

BEAN WITH BACON SOUP

INGREDIENTS:

- 2 tablespoons chopped onion
- 2 tablespoons bacon grease
- 2 cups tomato juice
- 2 cups water
- 1 cup milk or almond milk
- 3 tablespoons cornstarch
- 1 teaspoon salt
- ½ teaspoon onion powder
- 2 cups cooked navy beans
- 2 cups fried and crumbled bacon

INSTRUCTIONS:

1. In small pan, fry onion in grease until tender.
2. In 3-quart saucepan, mix tomato juice, water, milk, and cornstarch. Bring to boil. Add onion, salt, onion powder, beans, and bacon. Simmer 10 minutes.

Makes 2 quarts.

Katie Hershberger, *Apple Creek, OH*

STUFFED PEPPER SOUP

This tastes very similar to stuffed peppers, but it is easier to eat.

INGREDIENTS:

- 2 pounds ground beef
- 6 cups water
- 1 (28 ounce) can tomato sauce
- 1 (28 ounce) can diced tomatoes, undrained
- 2 cups chopped green pepper
- ¼ cup brown sugar
- 2 teaspoons salt
- 2 teaspoons beef bouillon granules
- 1 teaspoon pepper
- 2 cups cooked long grain rice
- Chopped fresh parsley (optional)

INSTRUCTIONS:

1. In Dutch oven over medium heat, cook beef until no longer pink, stirring often. Drain.
2. Stir in water, tomato sauce, tomatoes, green pepper, brown sugar, salt, bouillon, and pepper. Bring to boil. Reduce heat and simmer uncovered until peppers are tender, about 30 minutes.
3. Add cooked rice. Simmer uncovered 10 minutes longer.
4. If desired, sprinkle with parsley to serve.

Tip: If you don't have cooked rice, you can add 1 cup uncooked rice when you add the tomatoes before bringing it to boil.

Mrs. Amos Eicher, *Monroe, IN*

EASY CORN CHOWDER

INGREDIENTS:

- 5 to 6 slices bacon, chopped
- 1 medium onion, diced
- 3 medium potatoes, peeled and diced
- 1 cup water
- 3 cups 2% milk
- 1 (10 ounce) package frozen corn or corn cut from 5 to 6 ears fresh corn
- 2 teaspoons sugar
- ¼ cup unsalted butter
- 1½ teaspoons salt
- ¼ teaspoon pepper
- Chives, chopped (optional)

INSTRUCTIONS:

1. In large pot over medium heat, cook bacon, stirring occasionally until well cooked on all sides. Set bacon aside on paper towel.
2. Add chopped onion to bacon grease and sauté until tender, about 5 minutes.
3. Add potatoes and water. Cover and cook 8 to 10 minutes, stirring occasionally until fork tender.
4. Add 1½ cups milk and carefully use immersion blender to break down potatoes. You can also cool the soup a bit and put it into a blender and pulse to blend. Potatoes don't need to be pureed, just broken down a bit so that some texture remains.
5. Add remaining 1½ cups milk, corn, sugar, butter, salt, and pepper.
6. Bring to low simmer, reduce heat, and cook over low heat for 5 to 10 minutes until warmed through.
7. Serve topped with chives and bacon.

Ruby Joann Miller, *Auburn, KY*

CHEESY CHICKEN CHOWDER SOUP

INGREDIENTS:

- 3 cups chicken broth
- 2 cups diced potatoes
- 1 cup diced carrots
- 1 cup diced celery
- ½ cup diced onion
- ¾ teaspoon salt
- ¼ teaspoon pepper
- ¼ cup butter
- ½ cup flour
- 2 cups milk
- 2 cups shredded cheddar cheese
- 2 cups diced cooked chicken

INSTRUCTIONS:

1. In 4-quart saucepan, bring broth to boil. Reduce heat.
2. Add potatoes, carrots, celery, onion, salt, and pepper. Cover and simmer for 15 minutes or until vegetables are tender.
3. In saucepan, melt butter. Add flour and brown a little. Gradually stir in milk and cook over low heat until slightly thickened. Stir in cheese and cook until melted.
4. Add to vegetables. Stir in chicken. Cook and stir over low heat until heated through.

Ella E. Shetler, *West Salem, OH*

CHEESEBURGER SOUP

Nothing tastes better than a bowl of warm cheeseburger soup on a cold winter evening.

INGREDIENTS:

- 4 cups chicken broth
- 1½ cups shredded carrots
- 4½ cups shredded potatoes
- 1 tablespoon chicken soup base
- ½ cup butter
- ¾ cup flour
- 4 cups milk
- 2 pounds ground beef
- ¾ cup chopped onion
- 2 teaspoons salt
- ½ teaspoon pepper
- 1 pound Velveeta cheese

INSTRUCTIONS:

1. In 4-quart saucepan, mix chicken broth, carrots, potatoes, and chicken soup base. Cook until vegetables are tender.
2. In small saucepan, melt butter. Add flour and let it brown a little. Slowly add milk and heat until thick, stirring constantly. Add to cooked vegetables.
3. In skillet, fry ground beef and onion together. Season with salt and pepper. Add to soup.
4. Add Velveeta cheese and stir until melted. Do not boil.

Makes 4 quarts.

Anna Swartzentruber, *West Salem, OH*

COUNTRY HAM AND POTATO SOUP

INGREDIENTS:

3 cups diced potatoes
½ cup diced carrots
½ cup chopped onion
1½ cups water
1 tablespoon chicken bouillon
Salt and pepper to taste
2 cups milk
1 cup sour cream
2 tablespoons flour
½ pound ham, cubed
1 tablespoon parsley flakes
Velveeta cheese

INSTRUCTIONS:

1. In large pot, cook potatoes, carrots, and onion in water. Add bouillon, salt, and pepper. Cook until tender. Add 1 cup milk.
2. In bowl, combine sour cream and flour. Add remaining 1 cup milk.
3. Gradually add mixture to soup base. Add ham and cook over low heat, stirring constantly until thickened.
4. Add parsley and as much cheese as desired, stirring until melted.

Emma Byler, *New Wilmington, PA*

CHILI SOUP

INGREDIENTS:

- 2 pounds ground beef
- ½ cup chopped onion
- 1 rounded tablespoon chili powder
- 1½ tablespoons salt
- ½ teaspoon pepper
- 1⅓ cups flour
- 6 cups water
- 1 can kidney or chili beans, drained
- 2 cups tomato juice
- Ketchup (optional)
- 1 cup brown sugar

INSTRUCTIONS:

1. In saucepan, brown beef with onion, chili powder, salt, and pepper.
2. Remove from heat and mix in flour.
3. Return to heat and add water. Bring to boil.
4. Add beans and tomato juice. Add ketchup to taste if desired. Stir in brown sugar.
5. It is ready when heated through, or simmer for a while to develop richer taste.

Ella Arlene Yoder, *Arcola, IL*

ADDING *to* *the* FEAST

When thou hast eaten and art full, then thou shalt bless the Lord *thy God for the good land which he hath given thee.*

~ Deuteronomy 8:10

LETTUCE DRESSING

This dressing is used on lettuce salads in Amish weddings.

INGREDIENTS:

- 1 pint sweet cream
- 1 pint sour cream
- ¾ cup salad dressing (like Miracle Whip)
- ¾ cup sugar
- 2 tablespoons mustard
- 1 tablespoon salt

INSTRUCTIONS:

1. Mix all ingredients together well.
2. Drizzle over lettuce or mix into salad.

Katie Gingerich, *Dalton, OH*

SWEET AND SOUR DRESSING

INGREDIENTS:

- 1 cup vegetable oil
- 1 cup sugar
- 1 tablespoon salad dressing (like Miracle Whip)
- 1 medium onion, grated
- ¼ cup water
- ¼ cup vinegar
- 2 tablespoons mustard
- 1 teaspoon salt
- 1 teaspoon celery seed
- ¼ teaspoon pepper

INSTRUCTIONS:

1. Blend oil and sugar well. Add salad dressing and onion, mixing well.
2. Add water and vinegar. Mix in mustard, salt, celery seed, and pepper. Mix well.
3. This salad dressing keeps for a long time.

Mattie J. Gingerich, *Dalton, OH*

CAULIFLOWER AND BROCCOLI SALAD

INGREDIENTS:

- 1 small head cauliflower, chopped
- 1 head broccoli, chopped
- 1 pound bacon, fried and crumbled
- 4 cups grated cheddar cheese
- 1½ cups sour cream
- 1½ cups salad dressing or mayonnaise
- 1 scant cup sugar
- 1 teaspoon salt
- ½ package ranch dressing mix

INSTRUCTIONS:

1. In bowl, combine cauliflower, broccoli, bacon, and cheese.
2. In another bowl, mix sour cream, salad dressing, sugar, salt, and ranch dressing mix. Stir into vegetable mixture until well coated.
3. Chill.
4. Best made a day ahead.

Sarah Brenneman, *Newcomerstown, OH*

CABBAGE SALAD

INGREDIENTS:

- 1 small head cabbage, shredded
- ½ cup chopped green pepper
- ½ cup chopped onion
- 3 tablespoons mayonnaise
- 2 tablespoons vinegar
- 1 tablespoon sugar or sweetener of choice
- ¼ teaspoon salt
- 4 strips bacon, cooked and crumbled

INSTRUCTIONS:

1. In large bowl, combine cabbage, green pepper, and onion.
2. In small bowl, mix mayonnaise, vinegar, sugar, and salt. Pour over cabbage and toss to coat.
3. Cover and chill for at least 4 hours.
4. Stir in bacon just before serving.

Makes 6 to 8 servings.

Carolyn Lambright, *Lagrange, IN*

POTATO SALAD

INGREDIENTS:

- 12 cups cooked and shredded potatoes
- 12 hard-boiled eggs, shredded
- 1½ cups chopped onion
- 1½ cups diced celery
- 3 cups mayonnaise
- 3 tablespoons vinegar
- 3 tablespoons mustard
- 4 teaspoons salt
- 2 cups sugar
- ½ cup milk

INSTRUCTIONS:

1. In large bowl, combine potatoes, eggs, onion, and celery.
2. In another bowl, mix mayonnaise, vinegar, mustard, salt, sugar, and milk. Pour over vegetables and stir to coat.
3. Tastes best after refrigerating overnight.

Mrs. Menno Schwartz, *Monroe, IN*

PLEASE
DO NOT

SWEET AND SOUR MACARONI SALAD

A very refreshing salad on a warm summer day.

INGREDIENTS:

- 1 pound pasta shells, cooked, drained, and cooled
- 2 cucumbers, diced
- 1 onion, diced
- 1 green pepper, diced
- 1 cup diced celery
- ¼ cup chopped parsley (optional)
- ½ cup vegetable oil
- ¾ cup sugar
- ¾ cup vinegar
- 1 can condensed tomato soup
- ½ teaspoon salt

INSTRUCTIONS:

1. In large bowl, combine pasta, cucumbers, onion, green pepper, celery, and parsley.
2. In small bowl, mix oil, sugar, vinegar, soup, and salt. Pour over pasta mixture and stir to coat well.
3. Chill.

Lorina Miller, *Mechanicstown, OH*

7-LAYER SALAD

INGREDIENTS:

3 cups salad dressing or Miracle Whip
1 tablespoon mustard
¼ cup sugar
1 tablespoon celery seed
1 head lettuce, cut up
1 onion, finely chopped
1 cup frozen peas
6 hard-boiled eggs, chopped
½ pound bacon, fried and crumbled
Cheese, shredded

INSTRUCTIONS:

1. In bowl, blend salad dressing, mustard, sugar, and celery seed.
2. In 9x13-inch pan, layer in order lettuce, onion, peas, eggs, bacon, dressing mixture, and cheese.
3. Chill several hours or overnight.

Mrs. Edna Weaver, *Big Prairie, OH*

CORN BREAD SALAD

CORN BREAD INGREDIENTS:

- 1 (8 ounce) box corn muffin mix
- 1 can chopped green chilies
- ⅛ teaspoon cumin
- ⅛ teaspoon oregano
- ⅛ teaspoon sage

DRESSING INGREDIENTS:

- 1 cup mayonnaise
- 1 cup sour cream
- 1 envelope or ⅛ cup ranch dressing mix

SALAD INGREDIENTS:

- 1 can black beans, drained
- 1 cup whole kernel corn
- 3 medium tomatoes, chopped
- 1 cup chopped bell pepper
- 1 cup chopped onion
- 2 cups shredded cheddar cheese
- 10 slices bacon, fried and crumbled

CORN BREAD INSTRUCTIONS:

1. In bowl, mix all ingredients together and bake according to muffin mix box.
2. Cool.

DRESSING INSTRUCTIONS:

In bowl, mix all ingredients well.

SALAD INSTRUCTIONS:

1. In 9x13-inch pan, crumble half of corn bread in bottom; top with half of black beans, dressing, corn, tomatoes, bell pepper, onion, cheese, and bacon.
2. Repeat layering with other half of corn bread, salad ingredients, and dressing.
3. Chill before serving.

Salomie E. Glick, *Howard, PA*

TOMATO-CUCUMBER SALAD

INGREDIENTS:

- 2 tomatoes, peeled and cubed
- 2 cucumbers, peeled and sliced
- ¼ cup chopped onion
- ½ cup cubed cheese
- 2 tablespoons mayonnaise
- 1 teaspoon salt
- ½ teaspoon vinegar
- 2 teaspoons sugar

INSTRUCTIONS:

1. In bowl, combine tomatoes, cucumbers, onion, and cheese.
2. In small bowl, blend mayonnaise, salt, vinegar, and sugar. Pour over tomato mixture and stir to coat.

Moses and Leah Renno, *Jackson, OH*

SCALLOPED PINEAPPLE

INGREDIENTS:

- 8 slices white bread
- 4 cups sugar
- ½ cup melted butter
- 6 eggs, beaten
- 2 cups milk
- 2 (20 ounce) cans crushed pineapple

INSTRUCTIONS:

1. Preheat oven to 350 degrees.
2. In bowl, tear bread into pieces then stir in sugar. Pour melted butter over bread and sugar and mix.
3. Stir in beaten eggs. Add milk and crushed pineapple, juice and all.
4. Pour into 10x15-inch greased pan.
5. Bake immediately for about 1 hour until set and nicely browned on top.
6. Serve as soon as possible.

Elsie Miller, *Arthur, IL*

HARVARD BEETS

A family favorite often enjoyed at the noon meal.

INGREDIENTS:

- ½ cup sugar
- 1 teaspoon salt
- 1 tablespoon cornstarch
- ½ cup vinegar
- ¼ cup water
- 3 cups cooked and diced red beets
- 2 tablespoons butter

INSTRUCTIONS:

1. In saucepan, mix sugar, salt, and cornstarch. Add vinegar and water. Stir until smooth. Cook for 5 minutes.
2. Add beets to sauce and let stand 30 minutes.
3. Just before serving, bring to boil and add butter.

Lovina J. Gingerich, *Dalton, OH*

SWISS CREAMY CORN

INGREDIENTS:

- 3 tablespoons butter
- ½ cup chopped onion
- 2½ cups corn
- ½ cup milk
- ½ cup sweet cream
- 4 to 6 slices Velveeta cheese

INSTRUCTIONS:

1. In saucepan, melt butter. Add onion and cook until soft. Add corn, heating to boil.
2. Add milk and cream; return to boil.
3. Add cheese. Turn off heat and serve hot.

Lovina J. Gingerich, *Dalton, OH*

OLD-FASHIONED GREEN BEANS

INGREDIENTS:

6 strips bacon, cut into ½-inch pieces

3 pounds fresh green beans

3 tablespoons brown sugar

½ cup water

INSTRUCTIONS:

1. In large skillet, cook bacon until tender and crisp. Add beans, brown sugar, and water.
2. Simmer 15 minutes.

Anna D. Byler, *Spartansburg, PA*

SCALLOPED CORN

INGREDIENTS:

- 1 (14.75 ounce) can creamed corn
- 1 cup milk
- 2 large eggs
- ¼ teaspoon nutmeg (optional)
- 5 tablespoons butter, melted
- Salt and pepper to taste
- 1 sleeve saltine crackers, crushed

INSTRUCTIONS:

1. Preheat oven to 350 degrees.
2. In large mixing bowl, combine corn, milk, eggs, nutmeg, and 3 tablespoons melted butter. Salt and pepper to taste. Stir in ⅔ cracker crumbs.
3. Pour into greased 2-quart baking dish.
4. Bake for 20 minutes.
5. Stir. Continue to bake 35 minutes.
6. In small bowl, combine remaining cracker crumbs with 2 tablespoons melted butter. Toss to coat crumbs.
7. Sprinkle over corn and bake 5 minutes or until golden.

Anna M. Weaver, *Mertztown, PA*

CORN OYSTERS

I still have fond memories of when my mother made these for me at home over thirty years ago. Now I make them for my family.

INGREDIENTS:

- 1 cup creamed corn
- ⅓ cup flour
- 1 teaspoon baking powder
- ½ teaspoon salt
- Ketchup

INSTRUCTIONS:

1. Mix corn, flour, baking powder, and salt.
2. Drop by ¼-cup scoop into hot oil. Fry until lightly browned on both sides.
3. Serve with ketchup.

Elizabeth Esh, *Paradise, PA*

GLORIFIED BAKED BEANS

INGREDIENTS:

- 1½ pounds ground beef
- 1 medium onion, chopped
- 1 pound bacon, fried and crumbled (save grease)
- Salt, pepper, and garlic powder to taste
- Dash liquid smoke
- 1 pound smoked sausage links, sliced
- 1 (16 ounce) can butter beans, drained
- 1 (16 ounce) can lima beans, drained
- 56 ounces Bush's baked beans with brown sugar and bacon
- 1 scant cup brown sugar
- 2 tablespoons mustard
- 2 tablespoons vinegar
- 2 tablespoons Worcestershire sauce
- 2 cups ketchup
- 2 cups barbecue sauce

INSTRUCTIONS:

1. In skillet, fry beef and onion in bacon grease. Season with salt, pepper, and garlic powder to taste. Add liquid smoke.
2. Pour into large slow cooker.
3. Mix in sausage, butter beans, lima beans, and baked beans.
4. In bowl, combine brown sugar, mustard, vinegar, Worcestershire sauce, ketchup, and barbecue sauce, mixing well.
5. Pour over meat and bean mixture. Stir in bacon.
6. Cook in slow cooker on low for 3 hours.
7. Alternatively, you can place ingredients in roasting pan and bake at 350 degrees for 1 hour.

Brenda Graber, *Hamptonville, NC*

MAKE-AHEAD MASHED POTATOES

INGREDIENTS:

5 pounds potatoes
1 (8 ounce) package cream cheese
8 ounces sour cream
1 teaspoon minced onion flakes
Milk
Salt to taste
½ cup butter, melted

INSTRUCTIONS:

1. Preheat oven to 350 degrees.
2. Peel potatoes and boil in salted water until soft. Drain.
3. Add cream cheese, sour cream, and onion flakes.
4. Mash potatoes. Add enough milk for desired consistency and salt to taste. (You can refrigerate for 24 hours before baking.)
5. Spread in buttered 9x13-inch pan.
6. Bake for 1 hour.
7. Drizzle melted butter over top when ready to serve.

Mrs. Andy (Malinda) Gingerich, *Hartford, KS*

PARSLEY POTATOES

INGREDIENTS:

- 10 medium potatoes, cubed
- 2 teaspoons garlic salt
- 2 tablespoons parsley flakes
- ¼ cup butter, melted
- ½ cup fried and crumbled bacon
- 1 cup shredded cheddar cheese

INSTRUCTIONS:

1. Preheat oven to 350 degrees.
2. Put potatoes in baking dish and sprinkle with garlic salt and parsley. Drizzle with butter and sprinkle with bacon.
3. Cover and bake for 1 hour.
4. Sprinkle with cheese and return to oven until cheese is melted and potatoes are tender.

Mrs. Joseph Beiler, *Woodward, PA*

OVEN FRENCH FRIES

INGREDIENTS:

- 4 large potatoes, cut into long sticks ⅜-inch wide
- 1 quart iced water
- ¼ cup olive oil
- Salt

INSTRUCTIONS:

1. Place potato sticks in large bowl with iced water and refrigerate for 15 minutes or more.
2. Preheat oven to 400 degrees.
3. Drain and pat dry with paper towels.
4. Put potato sticks in large storage bag and drizzle with olive oil. Close bag and shake until evenly coated.
5. Spread on large baking sheet. Bake for 40 minutes, tossing with fork every 10 minutes.
6. Salt well, and serve with ketchup.

Esther Troyer, *Walhonding, OH*

POTATO BALLS

INGREDIENTS:

- ¼ cup chopped onion
- ½ cup diced celery
- ¼ cup butter
- 4 cups mashed potatoes
- 3 cups breadcrumbs
- 2 eggs
- 1 teaspoon salt
- ½ teaspoon pepper
- Milk
- ¼ cup melted butter

INSTRUCTIONS:

1. Preheat oven to 375 degrees.
2. In saucepan, sauté onion and celery in ¼ cup butter until soft.
3. Add potatoes, breadcrumbs, eggs, salt, pepper, and just enough milk to moisten. Form balls.
4. Arrange balls of mixture on baking sheet.
5. Pour ¼ cup melted butter over all.
6. Bake uncovered for 20 minutes.

Emma Byler, *New Wilmington, PA*

CHEESY AMISH POTATO CASSEROLE

This popular dish is sometimes called Funeral Potatoes because it is easy to make for potluck dinners of any sort, including a funeral lunch. But it is served all the time in Amish households with a meal. Cheesy potatoes in any form have always been a favorite of mine. Give this a try; I think your family will ask for more!

INGREDIENTS:

- 8 to 10 cups shredded potatoes, fresh or frozen
- 2½ cups milk
- 2 tablespoons butter
- ½ teaspoon salt (optional)
- 2 tablespoons flour
- ½ teaspoon pepper (optional)
- ½ cup chopped onion
- 2 cups shredded cheese

INSTRUCTIONS:

1. Preheat oven to 350 degrees.
2. Grease 9x13-inch baking dish.
3. Let potatoes thaw if you are using frozen. Microwave works fine.
4. Dump everything into large bowl and, using clean hands or big spoon, mix it all up thoroughly. (Great activity to get your kids into!)
5. Press it all into greased baking dish.
6. Bake for 50 to 60 minutes, until golden brown and bubbly.

OPTIONAL TOPPING:

To make it authentically Amish, add crushed-cornflake-and-butter topping. (Crunch up enough cornflakes to make ½ cup and add 2 tablespoons melted butter. Mix it up, then sprinkle on casserole before baking.) Yummy!

NOTES:

- I recommend a 30-ounce bag of frozen hash brown potatoes, shredded or diced. But if you have time, precooked fresh potatoes also work.
- If you'd like to try something different, switch out milk for can of condensed cream of chicken or mushroom soup and cup of sour cream.
- If you don't have fresh onion on hand, you can use frozen or even dehydrated onions in a pinch. Once baked, nobody will be the wiser!

Anne Blackburne, *Ohio*

AMISH DRESSING

INGREDIENTS:

12 to 14 eggs
¾ gallon whole milk
4 cups chicken broth
2 tablespoons salt
2 tablespoons chicken base
1 teaspoon pepper
4 cups diced cooked potatoes
4 cups diced celery
4 cups diced cooked carrots
4 cups diced cooked chicken
Dried bread cubes from approximately 4 loaves

INSTRUCTIONS:

1. Preheat oven to 325 degrees.
2. In 13-quart bowl, beat eggs.
3. Stir in milk and broth. Mix in salt, chicken base, and pepper. Add potatoes, celery, carrots, and chicken.
4. Add dried bread cubes, mixing in enough until you have a very moist mixture that is not soupy.
5. Spread into greased roaster pan.
6. Bake for 1 to 1½ hours.

Mrs. Joseph Miller, *Navarre, OH*

CHICKEN BONE BROTH

This broth is very nutritious and full of minerals. To pull even more minerals from the bones, add a splash of vinegar or a tablespoon of Real Salt before simmering.

INGREDIENTS:

2 onions
4 cloves garlic
3 stalks celery
Chicken backs and bones to fill 6-quart slow cooker

INSTRUCTIONS:

1. Put everything in slow cooker and cover with cold water. Turn on low for 10 to 12 hours or up to 24 hours.
2. Strain and discard bones.
3. Drink, use in soup, freeze, or can broth.
4. To can, fill quart jars, tighten on 2-piece lids, and pressure cook at 10 pounds for 25 minutes.

Note: You can keep a bag in your freezer to collect bones and vegetable scraps until you have enough to fill the slow cooker.

Esther Troyer, *Walhonding, OH*

HOMEMADE NOODLES

INGREDIENTS:

2 cups egg yolks
1 egg
1½ cups boiling water
Flour

INSTRUCTIONS:

1. Use scale and weigh medium-sized (8 quart) mixing bowl.
2. Into bowl, beat egg yolks and whole egg well. Mix in boiling water.
3. Place bowl on scale and add flour, mixing until it reaches 5 pounds dough. (Subtract original weight of bowl.) Mix well.
4. Let dough rest 15 minutes.
5. Roll dough out as thin as you wish with pasta machine.
6. Cut dough in strips of desired width.
7. Cover table with cloth. Lay noodles out on cloth and cover with second cloth. Let sit to dry in warm place for 5 to 7 days.
8. Store noodles in airtight container.

Mrs. Moses Swarey, *Mt. Ayr, IA*

BROWN BUTTERED NOODLES

When I was growing up, my dad would boil up a big—and I mean BIG!—pot of egg noodles and butter, salt, and pepper them generously before dishing them up. This was a favorite of my children, and I still love it today if my stomach is a bit upset or if I just need comfort food. The Amish have a slight twist on this old favorite. They first brown the butter, which does something magical and mysterious to the old standard, causing it to become fragrant and delectable!

INGREDIENTS:

- Egg noodles
- Real butter, salted is best
- Salt

INSTRUCTIONS:

1. In large saucepan, boil batch of egg noodles—as many as your family needs.
2. When noodles are done, drain them well and put them into big bowl.
3. During final 10 minutes or so of noodle cooking, brown butter: Put butter into saucepan. Use 1 or 2 sticks, based on how many noodles you made. You'll want butter to coat noodles uniformly. Don't be stingy.
4. On medium heat, bring butter to slow, rolling boil. It will start to sputter and spit, and it will eventually froth and foam. After a while (don't leave stove—a while could be a short while or a few minutes) you'll notice foam turning a bit brown. Move it aside with spatula and peek beneath at butter. It starts out butter yellow, but it will turn caramel brown.
5. Once this color is achieved, pour butter over noodles, salting to taste and stirring to coat.
6. This is one of the easiest and most satisfying things I've ever made.

Anne Blackburne, *Ohio*

AMISH NOODLES

This makes a large batch of noodles for a crowd.

INGREDIENTS:

- 1 pound butter
- 6 (48 ounce) cans or 9 quarts chicken broth
- 3 quarts plus 1 cup water
- ¾ cup chicken base
- 2½ tablespoons salt
- 1 teaspoon pepper
- 50 ounces cream of mushroom soup
- 1½ pounds Velveeta cheese
- 5 pounds egg noodles

INGREDIENTS FOR SMALLER BATCH:

- ½ cup butter
- 1 quart chicken broth
- 1 quart water
- 4 teaspoons chicken base
- 1½ teaspoons salt
- Pepper to taste
- 1 (10.5 ounce) can cream of mushroom soup
- ½ cup Velveeta cheese
- 1 pound egg noodles

INSTRUCTIONS:

1. In 20-quart kettle or canner, melt butter, browning it slightly. Add broth, water, chicken base, salt, and pepper. Bring to boil.
2. Add soup and cheese, stirring until melted. Bring to boil.
3. Add noodles and return to boil.
4. Turn off heat. Cover and let sit for 2 to 3 hours.
5. Stir. Reheat if needed before serving.

Mrs. Joseph Miller, *Navarre, OH*

ZUCCHINI PATTIES

INGREDIENTS:

3 cups shredded zucchini
2 to 3 eggs
½ cup cracker crumbs
¼ cup oil
¾ cup chopped onion
1 teaspoon salt
½ teaspoon pepper

INSTRUCTIONS:

1. In bowl, mix zucchini, eggs, crackers, oil, and onion. Season with salt and pepper.
2. Form into patties.
3. Fry in hot, greased skillet.
4. Good served with salad dressing and fresh pickles or tomatoes.

Lena Troyer, *Redding, IA*

STEWED TOMATOES

Another favorite recipe I grew up with that you'll find on Amish tables is stewed tomatoes. I adore these! This is my dad's recipe, and my siblings and I are carrying on his tradition.

Some people will use fresh tomatoes from their garden for this, first scalding them in boiling water then dunking them into an ice bath to make them easy to peel. Or they may have cans of homegrown tomatoes they've put up for the winter and use those. Sadly, I am not one of those people. I buy a 28-ounce can of peeled, whole tomatoes. Choose your favorite brand. And I proceed from there.

INGREDIENTS:

- 1 (28 ounce) can peeled, whole tomatoes
- ½ stick butter
- ½ sleeve Ritz crackers, crushed
- ¼ cup milk
- ¼ cup chopped onion (Dehydrated or frozen onions may be substituted. If you use dehydrated, you only need a couple of tablespoons.)
- 1 teaspoon sugar
- Dash salt and pepper (optional)

INSTRUCTIONS:

1. Do not drain tomatoes. Cut them into smaller chunks. (I do this right in the can.)
2. In 2-quart saucepan, melt butter to coat bottom of pan.
3. Add tomatoes, crackers, milk, onion, sugar, salt, and pepper. Let simmer. Stir occasionally. You don't want to boil this; just simmer nicely for about 15 to 20 minutes as tomatoes cook down and all ingredients make friends with one another. Be patient; if your heat is too high, you'll scorch it and lose the whole thing. When done, it will look like chunky glop, but it's delicious!

Anne Blackburne, *Ohio*

SWEET POTATO SOUFFLÉ

SOUFFLÉ INGREDIENTS:

- 3 large sweet potatoes, peeled, cooked, and mashed
- 2 eggs, beaten
- ½ cup sugar
- ⅓ cup melted butter
- 1 teaspoon vanilla
- 1 can evaporated milk

TOPPING INGREDIENTS:

- 1 cup brown sugar
- 1 cup chopped nuts
- ⅓ cup melted butter
- ⅓ cup flour

SOUFFLÉ INSTRUCTIONS:

1. Preheat oven to 350 degrees.
2. In bowl, mix sweet potatoes, eggs, sugar, melted butter, vanilla, and milk.
3. Spread in baking dish and bake for 45 minutes or until set.
4. Add topping and bake for 10 minutes or until bubbly.

TOPPING INSTRUCTIONS:

In bowl, mix all ingredients then pour over hot casserole.

Salomie E. Glick, *Howard, PA*

BUTTERNUT SQUASH CASSEROLE

INGREDIENTS:

- 6 cups cubed butternut squash
- ¼ cup chopped onion
- ¼ cup butter
- ¼ teaspoon pepper
- 2 teaspoons parsley flakes
- 1 teaspoon salt
- ¼ cup milk or cream
- Cheese, shredded

INSTRUCTIONS:

1. Preheat oven to 350 degrees.
2. Put butternut squash in 9x13-inch baking pan.
3. In small skillet, sauté onion in butter until tender. Add pepper, parsley, salt, and milk. Pour over squash.
4. Cover and bake for 1½ hours.
5. Shortly before it's done, in last 10 to 15 minutes, uncover and sprinkle with cheese.

Danny and Ruth Detweiler, *Tazewell, VA*

VEGETABLE PIZZA

CRUST INGREDIENTS:

- 1 tablespoon yeast
- ¼ cup sugar
- 2 cups flour
- 4 pinches salt
- 1 egg
- 6 tablespoons butter

DRESSING INGREDIENTS:

- 1 (8 ounce) package cream cheese
- ¾ cup mayonnaise
- 1 tablespoon ranch dressing powder

TOPPING INGREDIENTS:

- 3 cups chopped tomatoes
- 2 cups finely chopped cauliflower
- 2 cups shredded cheese
- 2 cups shredded carrots
- 1 cup finely chopped celery

CRUST INSTRUCTIONS:

1. Preheat oven to 350 degrees.
2. Combine all ingredients and spread on baking sheet.
3. Bake for 30 minutes.
4. Cool.

DRESSING INSTRUCTIONS:

1. Blend all ingredients until smooth.
2. Spread over crust.

TOPPING INGREDIENTS INSTRUCTIONS:

1. Sprinkle ingredients over dressing.
2. Chill.

Katie E. Stoltzfus, *Charlotte CH., VA*

CHEESY BEAN DIP

INGREDIENTS:

- 4 tablespoons butter
- ¼ cup flour
- ½ teaspoon salt
- ¼ teaspoon red pepper
- 2 cups milk
- ½ pound white Velveeta cheese
- 1 teaspoon Worcestershire sauce
- 1 can refried beans

INSTRUCTIONS:

1. In saucepan, melt butter; blend in flour, salt, and pepper.
2. Add milk and stir until thickened. Add cheese and Worcestershire sauce.
3. Spread beans in small pan.
4. Pour cheese sauce on top.
5. Serve with tortilla chips.

Sharon Mishler, *LaGrange, IN*

JALAPEÑO POPPER DIP

INGREDIENTS:

- 2 (8 ounce) packages cream cheese, softened
- 2 cups sour cream
- ½ cup Miracle Whip salad dressing
- 4 to 6 jalapeño peppers, seeded and chopped
- 1½ cups shredded cheddar cheese
- ¼ cup chopped onion
- 1 cup crushed Ritz crackers
- ½ cup grated Parmesan cheese
- ¼ cup butter, melted
- 2 teaspoons dried parsley flakes

INSTRUCTIONS:

1. Preheat oven to 350 degrees.
2. In medium bowl, blend cream cheese, sour cream, and salad dressing. Mix in jalapeño peppers, cheddar cheese, and onion, stirring well.
3. Spread in 9-inch round baking pan.
4. In bowl, mix crackers, Parmesan cheese, melted butter, and parsley. Spread over dip.
5. Bake 20 minutes or until hot.
6. Serve with your favorite crackers.

Kathryn Schwartz, *Berne, IN*

MY AMISH NEIGHBORS

When I'm not writing, gardening, or walking with my much-beloved Labrador Ms. Ellie, I'm often visiting my Amish neighbors. I admire their desire to live a devout Christian life that strives to honor God. The Amish are excellent cooks and bakers and live such peaceful lifestyles, despite the hard work and deep commitments of their steadfast faith. And some of my attraction to the Amish and Mennonite community came from the wonderful recipes shared with me over the years.

I've traveled to many communities in various states and made wonderful lifelong friends, but it is home in northeastern Kentucky where I find much of the inspiration for each of my books. The Amish of northeastern Kentucky are of Swiss descent, and most come from larger areas such as Indiana, Michigan, Missouri, and New York. Signature for the Swiss Amish of northern Kentucky are their open-top buggies, different styles of clothing in hues of blue, tan, and charcoal black, strong conservative Ordnung (rules of the church), and Swiss dialect. Many of my neighbors can speak four languages to some degree.

Traditional fare consists of loaves of bread, pies, pork, and noodles. Meals are often served with water and coffee, but on occasion there's homemade lemonade, and Meadow tea is a summertime favorite. Peanut butter spread is not on every table, and pon hoss is not so bad as long as you don't ask how it's made. Then again, asking is how I learned to make my own trail bologna.

Many Amish dishes are similar to the comfort foods of my Appalachian upbringing. Vegetables are grown from the land, and the best cuts of meat come straight from the farm. Our dear friend Adam still ranks number one in pulled pork, and it's often a family or community event to butcher and preserve meat together.

Canning peaches or sausage is often done with others on a "Sister's Day." Many also call this "Ladies Day." It's a sight to see hundreds of jars of preserved foods lining tables. It was during a work event where the proceeds were donated to the local school funds that I was blessed to tag along to help serve while my husband and son-in-law helped the men. I've eaten my share of cinnamon rolls, but this was where I tried my first strawberry roll. They are a special twist on the Amish cinnamon roll and much sought after.

Oftentimes I've tried to disappear behind my writing desk for a deadline and have been stirred by a knock at the door to discover a pan of warm cinnamon rolls slathered in brown sugar and pecans or a plate of fresh cookies is being delivered by young hands.

Faith, family, and community are very essential to the Amish, and food is a labor of love. Sharing a meal or a snack is a great way to fellowship. A midweek break, where friends gather to sing or visit, always consists of wonderful snack foods. It may be popcorn, homemade ice cream and brownies, or potato chips and soda pop. There's something to be said about sitting next to a warm fire, a cup of warm Ganoderma (4-in-1 coffee) in hand, while catching up with friends.

Living among Old Order Amish has always given me kind fellowship and a greater sense of community. It has also made me a better baker. An Amish kitchen is one that is always ready to serve, and as my dear friend Esther says, "You never know who might stop by." So there is often a sweet dish waiting. Her blackberry crumble hits the spot for sure.

I've shared a few recipes from my dear Amish friends of Kentucky.

MINDY STEELE

Mindy lives in Kentucky with her husband, where she enjoys her four grown children, grandchildren, hiking, and gardening.

SATISFYING *the* SWEET TOOTH

How sweet are thy words unto my taste!
yea, sweeter than honey to my mouth!
~ Psalm 119:103

DATE PUDDING

PUDDING INGREDIENTS:

1 cup boiling water
1 cup chopped dates
1 cup brown sugar
1 teaspoon baking powder
1 teaspoon baking soda
1 egg
1 cup flour
1 tablespoon butter
Butterscotch sauce
Whipped cream
Banana, sliced
Nuts, chopped

BUTTERSCOTCH SAUCE INGREDIENTS:

1 cup butter
4 cups water
3 cups brown sugar
¾ cup Clear Jel
1 cup water
Salt to taste
1 teaspoon vanilla

PUDDING INSTRUCTIONS:

1. Preheat oven to 325 degrees.
2. In bowl, pour boiling water over dates. Let cool.
3. Add brown sugar, baking powder, baking soda, egg, flour, and butter to dates. Mix well and pour into buttered baking dish.
4. Bake for 25 to 30 minutes.
5. Top individual servings with butterscotch sauce, whipped cream, sliced banana, and nuts.

BUTTERSCOTCH SAUCE INSTRUCTIONS:

1. In saucepan, bring butter, 4 cups water, and brown sugar to boil.
2. In bowl, mix Clear Jel with 1 cup water. Add to sauce and return to boil, stirring constantly until thickened. Add salt and vanilla.

Katie Gingerich, *Dalton, OH*

APPLE GRUNT

GRUNT INGREDIENTS:

- ½ cup sugar
- 2 tablespoons shortening
- 1 egg
- ½ teaspoon baking soda
- ½ cup sour milk or buttermilk
- ½ teaspoon vanilla
- 1 cup flour
- 1 teaspoon baking powder
- ½ teaspoon salt
- 1½ cups sliced apples

CRUMB TOPPING INGREDIENTS:

- 6 tablespoons brown sugar
- 1½ tablespoons flour
- 1½ tablespoons butter
- ½ teaspoon cinnamon

GRUNT INSTRUCTIONS:

1. Preheat oven to 375 degrees.
2. In mixing bowl, cream sugar and shortening. Add egg and beat well. Add baking soda to sour milk and stir into first mixture. Add vanilla.
3. In another bowl, sift flour, baking powder, and salt. Add to first mixture.
4. Fold in apples and blend well.
5. Pour into greased, shallow baking dish.
6. Sprinkle topping over batter.
7. Bake for 35 to 40 minutes.
8. Serve hot with milk.

Makes 4 to 6 servings.

CRUMB TOPPING INSTRUCTIONS:

Mix all ingredients together until crumbly.

Judith Miller, *Fredericktown, OH*

CARROT CAKE

INGREDIENTS:

- 1 cup sugar
- 1½ cups butter
- ½ cup honey
- 4 eggs, separated
- 2½ cups shredded carrots
- 2 cups whole grain flour
- 2 teaspoons baking powder
- 1½ teaspoons baking soda
- ½ teaspoon salt
- 2 teaspoons cinnamon
- ½ cup chopped nuts

INSTRUCTIONS:

1. Preheat oven to 350 degrees.
2. Grease 9x13-inch cake pan.
3. In mixing bowl, cream together sugar and butter. Add honey and egg yolks, mixing well. Stir in carrots.
4. Add flour, baking powder, baking soda, salt, and cinnamon, mixing well. Stir in nuts.
5. In bowl, beat egg whites then fold into mixture.
6. Spread into prepared pan.
7. Bake for 35 minutes.
8. Frost as desired.

Grace Zimmerman, *Shiloh, OH*

LAZY WOMAN'S CAKE

INGREDIENTS:

- 2 cups sugar
- 3 cups flour
- 1 teaspoon salt
- 5 tablespoons cocoa powder
- 2 heaping teaspoons baking soda
- 1 scant cup oil
- 1 tablespoon vanilla
- 2 tablespoons vinegar
- 2 cups cold water

INSTRUCTIONS:

1. Preheat oven to 350 degrees.
2. Grease and flour 10x15-inch jelly roll pan.
3. In mixing bowl, blend all ingredients together.
4. Pour into prepared pan.
5. Bake for 30 minutes.
6. Frost as desired.
7. The batter also makes good cupcakes.

Lorene Schwartz, *Monroe, IN*
Susanne L. Wengerd, *Decatur, IN*

WET-BOTTOM SHOOFLY CAKE

INGREDIENTS:

- 3 cups brown sugar
- 1½ cups molasses
- 3 cups hot water
- 4 eggs
- 1 cup sugar
- 6 cups flour
- 1½ teaspoons baking soda
- 1 teaspoon salt
- 1 teaspoon cream of tartar
- 1 scant cup lard

INSTRUCTIONS:

1. Preheat oven to 400 degrees.
2. Grease 9x13-inch cake pan.
3. In bowl, beat together brown sugar, molasses, hot water, and eggs. Pour into cake pan.
4. In another bowl, mix sugar, flour, baking soda, salt, and cream of tartar then cut in lard until crumbly. Spread over liquid mixture.
5. Bake for 15 minutes at 400 degrees. Reduce to 350 degrees and bake for 25 minutes.

Menno and Esther Yoder, *Berlin, PA*

EASY-PEASY DUMP CAKE

As a young wife and mother, I often had occasion to attend events where I was expected to bring food. When strapped for time, I've always found this recipe to be quick and easy to prepare, and it's a guaranteed crowd-pleaser! Amish moms make this same recipe to take to community lunches and family dinners. This recipe smells heavenly while baking, and tastes just as good! Everyone will want the recipe.

INGREDIENTS:

1 can crushed pineapple, undrained

2 cans cherry pie filling

1 box white or yellow cake mix

1 stick butter

INSTRUCTIONS:

1. Preheat oven to 350 degrees.
2. Grease 9x13-inch glass or metal baking dish.
3. Dump pineapple with juice into bottom of baking dish, spreading evenly with spatula to cover bottom.
4. Dump pie filling in next, spreading it evenly over pineapple.
5. Dump cake mix over pie filling and pineapple, and spread it out evenly over fruit.
6. Cut up butter into thin slices and place squares all over top of cake mix.
7. Bake, uncovered, for 45 minutes to 1 hour, until golden and bubbly. As it bakes, cake mix absorbs fruit from below and butter from above.
8. Let cool somewhat before serving.

Note: Substitute any combination of pie filling and canned fruit you like, as well as any flavor cake mix, for your own delicious creation!

Anne Blackburne, *Ohio*

CHOCOLATE ZUCCHINI SHEET CAKE

CAKE INGREDIENTS:

- 2 cups sugar
- 1 cup vegetable oil
- 3 eggs
- 2½ cups flour
- ¼ cup cocoa powder
- 1 teaspoon baking soda
- ¼ teaspoon baking powder
- ¼ teaspoon salt
- ½ cup milk
- 2 cups shredded zucchini
- 1 tablespoon vanilla

FROSTING INGREDIENTS:

- ½ cup butter or margarine
- ¼ cup cocoa powder
- 6 tablespoons milk
- 1 pound powdered sugar
- 1 tablespoon vanilla

CAKE INSTRUCTIONS:

1. Preheat oven to 375 degrees.
2. Grease and flour 10x15-inch jelly roll pan.
3. In mixing bowl, combine sugar and oil. Add eggs, beating well.
4. Add flour, cocoa, baking soda, baking powder, and salt alternately with milk. Stir in zucchini and vanilla.
5. Pour into prepared baking sheet.
6. Bake for 25 minutes or until cake tests done.
7. While cake is baking, make frosting to spread over cake while still hot.

FROSTING INSTRUCTIONS:

Mix all together until smooth.

Emma Kurtz, *Smicksburg, PA*

NEVER-FAIL RED VELVET CAKE

CAKE INGREDIENTS:

- 2¼ cups sugar
- 1⅛ cups shortening
- 3 eggs
- 3 tablespoons Nestle Quik chocolate drink mix powder
- 3 tablespoons red food coloring
- 3 tablespoons water
- 1½ cups buttermilk
- 3⅜ cups cake flour
- ¾ teaspoon salt
- 1½ teaspoons baking soda
- 1½ teaspoons vinegar

FROSTING INGREDIENTS:

- 1 cup milk
- ¼ cup flour
- 1 cup sugar
- 1 cup shortening
- 1 teaspoon vanilla

CAKE INSTRUCTIONS:

1. Preheat oven to 350 degrees.
2. Grease and flour 10x15-inch jelly roll pan.
3. In mixing bowl, cream sugar, shortening, and eggs well.
4. In another bowl, drizzle Nestle Quik and food coloring into water. Add to creamed mixture. Add buttermilk.
5. Sift flour and salt together 3 times. Add to first mixture.
6. Dissolve baking soda in vinegar. Add to creamed mixture.
7. Spread batter into prepared jelly roll pan.
8. Bake for 25 to 30 minutes. Do not overbake!
9. Cool before frosting.

FROSTING INSTRUCTIONS:

1. In saucepan, cook milk and flour until thick. Cool well.
2. In bowl, beat together sugar, shortening, and vanilla. Add flour mixture and beat well.

Jesse and Rose Raber, *Montgomery, IN*

BEST RHUBARB CAKE DESSERT

LAYER 1 INGREDIENTS:

½ cup butter, diced
2 cups flour
2 tablespoons sugar

LAYER 2 INGREDIENTS:

6 egg yolks
2 cups sugar
3 tablespoons flour
¼ teaspoon salt
1 cup cream
5 cups chopped rhubarb

LAYER 3 INGREDIENTS:

6 egg whites
¾ cup sugar
2 teaspoons vanilla
Pinch salt

LAYER 1 INSTRUCTIONS:

1. Preheat oven to 350 degrees.
2. Mix all ingredients together until crumbly and pat into 9x13-inch pan.
3. Bake for 10 minutes.

LAYER 2 INSTRUCTIONS:

1. In bowl, mix egg yolks, sugar, flour, salt, and cream. Stir in rhubarb.
2. Spread over hot crust.
3. Bake for 40 to 45 minutes.

LAYER 3 INSTRUCTIONS:

1. In bowl, beat egg whites until stiffened. Add sugar, vanilla, and salt.
2. Spread over hot cake.
3. Bake 8 to 10 minutes until lightly browned. Watch closely.

Kristina Mast, *New Holstein, WI*
Mrs. Robert (Ruth) Mullet, *Danville, OH*
Samuel and Mary Mullet, *Bellville, OH*
Katie Yoder, *Sugarcreek, OH*

BUTTERSCOTCH PIE

INGREDIENTS:

1½ tablespoons butter
1 tablespoon flour
2 eggs, well beaten
1 cup brown sugar
¼ teaspoon salt
1¼ cups milk
1 teaspoon vanilla
1 unbaked pie shell

INSTRUCTIONS:

1. Preheat oven to 350 degrees.
2. In mixing bowl, cream butter and flour.
3. In another bowl, mix eggs and sugar. Add to butter mixture.
4. Add salt, milk, and vanilla.
5. Pour into unbaked pie shell.
6. Bake for 40 minutes until it rises.

Mrs. Joseph Miller, *Navarre, OH*

CHERRY CUSTARD PIE

INGREDIENTS:

2 tablespoons flour
1¼ cups brown sugar
Pinch salt
4 eggs, separated
2½ cups milk, scalded
1 teaspoon vanilla
1 teaspoon butter flavoring
Cherry pie filling
2 unbaked pie shells

INSTRUCTIONS:

1. Preheat oven to 450 degrees.
2. In mixing bowl, combine flour, sugar, salt, and egg yolks. Add scalded milk, vanilla, and butter flavoring.
3. In another bowl, beat egg whites then fold into mixture.
4. Put thin layer of pie filling in bottom of each pie shell.
5. Pour custard mixture over pie filling.
6. Bake at 450 degrees for 10 to 15 minutes. Reduce heat to 350 degrees and bake for 30 to 40 minutes until set.

Katie Gingerich, *Dalton, OH*

FRUIT PIE

The Fruit Pie recipe is perfect for any fruit. Apple, peach, or blueberry, this recipe is sure to become a family favorite.

INGREDIENTS:

2½ cups fruit filling of your choice
1 (9 inch) unbaked piecrust
½ cup sugar
3 tablespoons flour
1 cup sour cream
1 (3 ounce) package cream cheese
½ cup flour
¼ cup sugar
¼ cup cold butter, diced

INSTRUCTIONS:

1. Preheat oven to 425 degrees.
2. Put pie filling into unbaked piecrust.
3. In bowl, combine ½ cup sugar and 3 tablespoons flour. Add sour cream and cream cheese, blending well. Spread over pie filling.
4. In another bowl, use fork to mix ½ cup flour, ¼ cup sugar, and butter until crumbly. Spread over pie.
5. Bake at 425 degrees for 15 minutes. Reduce heat to 350 degrees and bake for 25 minutes.

Mindy Steele, *Kentucky*

RAISIN CREAM PIE

INGREDIENTS:

- 1 cup raisins
- 2 cups milk
- ¾ cup brown sugar
- 1 teaspoon cinnamon
- ½ teaspoon maple flavoring
- 2 eggs
- 1½ rounded tablespoons flour
- 1½ rounded tablespoons cornstarch
- 1 tablespoon butter
- 1 baked pie shell
- Whipped topping or whipped cream

INSTRUCTIONS:

1. In saucepan, cover raisins with water and cook for 5 minutes.
2. In another saucepan, bring milk to boil.
3. In bowl, mix sugar, cinnamon, maple flavoring, eggs, flour, and cornstarch. Add a little of mixture at a time to milk and cook, stirring until thickened.
4. Add butter and raisins (with cooking water).
5. Pour into baked pie shell. Cool.
6. Top with whipped topping.

Katie Gingerich, *Dalton, OH*

FRESH STRAWBERRY PIE

CRUST INGREDIENTS:

1 cup flour
2 tablespoons sugar
½ cup margarine or butter, melted

CREAM FILLING INGREDIENTS:

1 (8 ounce) package cream cheese, softened
1 (8 ounce) carton whipped topping
1 cup powdered sugar

STRAWBERRY FILLING INGREDIENTS:

2 cups water
1½ cups sugar
½ cup instant Clear Jel
¾ envelope strawberry Kool-Aid drink mix
¼ teaspoon salt
2 teaspoons vanilla
1¼ cups sliced fresh strawberries

CRUST INSTRUCTIONS:

1. Preheat oven to 350 degrees.
2. In bowl, mix flour, sugar, and melted margarine. Pat into pie pan.
3. Bake for 10 to 15 minutes. Cool.

CREAM FILLING INSTRUCTIONS:

1. In bowl, whip together cream cheese, whipped topping, and sugar until smooth.
2. Spread into cooled crust over bottom and up sides.

STRAWBERRY FILLING INSTRUCTIONS:

1. In bowl, blend water, sugar, Clear Jel, drink mix, salt, and vanilla, stirring until sugar is dissolved. Stir in strawberries.
2. Pour over cream filling.
3. Chill until set.

Henry and Lovina Shetler, *Pierpoint, OH*

OATMEAL PIE

INGREDIENTS:

- ¾ cup light corn syrup
- ½ cup sugar
- ½ cup brown sugar
- ½ cup butter, melted
- 1 teaspoon butter flavoring
- 1 teaspoon vanilla
- 4 eggs, beaten
- 2 cups milk
- ½ cup flaked coconut
- ½ cup oatmeal
- 2 (9 inch) unbaked pie shells

INSTRUCTIONS:

1. Preheat oven to 400 degrees.
2. Combine all ingredients and mix well.
3. Pour into unbaked pie shells.
4. Bake at 400 degrees for 10 minutes then at 350 degrees for 30 to 35 minutes or until pie tests done.

Lovina J. Gingerich, *Dalton, OH*

FRY PIES

PIE INGREDIENTS:

9 cups cake flour
2 tablespoons sugar
1 tablespoon salt
3 cups butter or shortening
2 cups water
1½ quarts pie filling of choice

GLAZE INGREDIENTS:

8 pounds powdered sugar
½ cup instant Clear Jel
1 teaspoon vanilla
2½ cups warm water

PIE INSTRUCTIONS:

1. In large mixing bowl, mix flour, sugar, salt, and shortening with hands until crumbs form. Add water and mix until soft dough forms.
2. Roll 2-to-2½-inch ball of dough into 6½-inch circle. Use round 6-inch plate or such to trim perfect circle.
3. Put ¼ to ⅓ cup pie filling on half of dough.
4. Moisten edges with wet fingertips to help create a better seal.
5. Fold remaining half of dough over top of filling.
6. Press edges together with fork.
7. Repeat steps 2 through 6 with remaining dough.
8. Fry pies, 2 to 3 at a time, in hot oil (350 degrees) for approximately 3 minutes or until lightly browned on both sides.
9. Place them on wire rack to cool for a few minutes, then drizzle with glaze.

GLAZE INSTRUCTIONS:

Mix all ingredients together until smooth.

Makes 30 pies.

Mrs. Joseph Miller, *Navarre, OH*

PUMPKIN ROLL

CAKE INGREDIENTS:

- 1 cup sugar
- 1 cup flour
- ½ teaspoon salt
- 1 teaspoon baking soda
- 2 teaspoons cinnamon
- ½ teaspoon pumpkin pie spice
- ⅔ cup pumpkin puree
- 3 eggs
- Powdered sugar

FILLING INGREDIENTS:

- 1 cup powdered sugar
- 1 tablespoon butter, softened
- 8 ounces cream cheese, softened
- 1 teaspoon vanilla

CAKE INSTRUCTIONS:

1. Preheat oven to 375 degrees.
2. Grease and flour or line with parchment paper 10x15-inch jelly roll pan.
3. In bowl, combine sugar, flour, salt, baking soda, cinnamon, and pumpkin pie spice.
4. Add puree and eggs. Don't overmix.
5. Spread into prepared pan.
6. Bake for 10 to 15 minutes.
7. Remove cake from oven and turn onto clean linen towel dusted with powdered sugar. Roll towel and cake together. Cool.
8. Gently unroll cooled cake; spread with filling and roll back up.
9. Set on plate and dust with powdered sugar.

FILLING INSTRUCTIONS:

Blend all filling ingredients together until smooth.

Jerry and Ida Petersheim, *Kenton, OH*

LATTICE FRUIT BARS

CRUST INGREDIENTS:

1 tablespoon yeast
1 tablespoon sugar
1 cup warm water
Doughnut mix

FILLING INGREDIENTS:

2 (8 ounce) packages cream cheese, softened
⅔ cup powdered sugar
1 egg yolk
1 teaspoon vanilla
Fruit filling of choice

CRUST INSTRUCTIONS:

1. In bowl, mix yeast, sugar, and water, stirring until dissolved. Add doughnut mix until smooth, stiff dough forms.
2. Let rise about 1 hour.
3. Roll half of dough onto 11x15-inch baking sheet.

FILLING INSTRUCTIONS:

1. Preheat oven to 350 degrees.
2. In mixing bowl, blend cream cheese, powdered sugar, egg yolk, and vanilla. Spread over dough.
3. Top with fruit filling.
4. Roll out remaining dough and cut strips, arranging them on top of fruit filling in lattice pattern. Bake for 30 minutes.
5. If desired, you can top baked crust with your favorite glaze.

Sarah Brenneman, *Newcomerstown, OH*

PEANUT BUTTER FUDGE BROWNIES

INGREDIENTS:

1 cup peanut butter
2 eggs
1 cup maple syrup or honey
1 teaspoon vanilla
½ cup cocoa powder
1 teaspoon baking soda
1 teaspoon salt
1 cup dark chocolate chips

INSTRUCTIONS:

1. Preheat oven to 325 degrees.
2. In bowl, blend peanut butter, eggs, maple syrup, and vanilla.
3. Add cocoa powder, baking soda, and salt. Mix well. Add chocolate chips.
4. Spread into greased 9x9-inch pan.
5. Bake for 20 minutes. Do not overbake.

Lizzie N. Christner, *Berne, IN*

ZUCCHINI BARS

BARS INGREDIENTS:

- 3 eggs
- 1 cup sugar
- 1 cup brown sugar
- 1 cup vegetable oil
- 2 cups flour
- 3 teaspoons cinnamon
- 1 teaspoon salt
- 2 teaspoons baking soda
- 1 teaspoon baking powder
- 2 cups grated zucchini

FROSTING INGREDIENTS:

- 4 ounces cream cheese, softened
- ½ cup butter, softened
- 2 cups powdered sugar
- 1 teaspoon vanilla
- ¼ to ½ cup chopped nuts

BARS INSTRUCTIONS:

1. Preheat oven to 350 degrees.
2. In mixing bowl, beat eggs. Add sugar, brown sugar, and oil, mixing well.
3. In another mixing bowl, sift together flour, cinnamon, salt, baking soda, and baking powder.
4. Add zucchini and dry mixture alternately to first mixture, mixing well.
5. Pour into greased and floured 9x13-inch pan.
6. Bake 30 minutes.

FROSTING INSTRUCTIONS:

1. In mixing bowl, cream together cream cheese and butter. Beat in powdered sugar and vanilla until smooth.
2. Spread over cooled zucchini bars.
3. Sprinkle with nuts.

Ella A. Hershberger, *Sullivan, OH*

BUTTERMILK COOKIES

This is a family favorite we also use for church dinners.

INGREDIENTS:

- 1 cup shortening
- 1 cup brown sugar
- 3 eggs
- 2 teaspoons baking powder
- 2 teaspoons baking soda
- 2 teaspoons vanilla
- ½ cup buttermilk or sour milk
- ¼ cup cream
- 4½ cups flour

INSTRUCTIONS:

1. Preheat oven to 350 degrees.
2. In mixing bowl, cream shortening and sugar. Add eggs, baking powder, baking soda, and vanilla; mix well.
3. Add buttermilk and cream alternately with flour until well blended.
4. Drop by teaspoonfuls onto well-greased cookie sheet.
5. Bake for 12 minutes.
6. Let sit for 5 minutes before removing from cookie sheet.

Note: To make sour milk, add 1 tablespoon vinegar to each cup of milk.

Mattie J. Gingerich, *Dalton, OH*

SECRET RECIPE CHOCOLATE CHIP COOKIES

INGREDIENTS:

½ cup quick oats
2¼ cups flour
1½ teaspoons baking soda
½ teaspoon salt
¼ teaspoon cinnamon
1 cup butter, softened
¾ cup sugar
¾ cup brown sugar
2 teaspoons vanilla
1 teaspoon lemon extract
2 eggs
3 cups chocolate chips
1½ cups chopped walnuts (optional)

INSTRUCTIONS:

1. Preheat oven to 350 degrees.
2. In bowl, combine oats, flour, baking soda, salt, and cinnamon.
3. In mixing bowl, cream butter, sugars, vanilla, and lemon extract. Add eggs and beat until fluffy. Stir in flour mixture.
4. Add chocolate chips and nuts.
5. Drop onto baking sheet in large spoonfuls.
6. Bake for 16 to 18 minutes. Do not overbake.

Abner and Amanda Miller,
Wisconsin Rapids, WI

CUTOUT COOKIES

COOKIE INGREDIENTS:

- 1½ cups sugar
- 2 cups butter (no substitute)
- 3 eggs, beaten
- 3 teaspoons vanilla
- 2 teaspoons salt
- 1 teaspoon baking soda
- 6 cups flour

ICING INGREDIENTS:

- 1 teaspoon salt
- ⅓ cup hot water
- 1¼ cups shortening
- 1 teaspoon vanilla
- Powdered sugar

COOKIE INSTRUCTIONS:

1. In mixing bowl, cream together sugar and butter. Add eggs and vanilla.
2. In another bowl, sift salt and baking soda with flour. Slowly add to creamed mixture.
3. Chill dough overnight.
4. Preheat oven to 350 degrees.
5. Roll dough out to ¼-to-⅜-inch thick. Use cookie cutters to cut out dough and place shapes on lightly floured cookie sheets.
6. Bake for about 8 minutes. Do not overbake.
7. Frost when cool.

ICING INSTRUCTIONS:

1. In bowl, dissolve salt in hot water; add shortening and vanilla.
2. Beat in 1 cup powdered sugar. Add more powdered sugar to reach the spreading consistency you want.
3. Beat until smooth.

Laura Miller, *Mount Vernon, OH*

MAPLE OATMEAL SANDWICH COOKIES

COOKIE INGREDIENTS:

- 1 cup shortening or butter
- 1 cup sugar
- 1 cup brown sugar
- 2 eggs
- 1 tablespoon milk
- 2 cups flour
- 1 teaspoon baking powder
- 1 teaspoon baking soda
- 1 teaspoon salt
- 2 cups quick oats
- 1 teaspoon vanilla
- 1 teaspoon maple flavoring

ICING INGREDIENTS:

- 1 (8 ounce) package cream cheese, softened
- 2 cups powdered sugar
- 1 stick butter, softened
- Maple flavoring

COOKIE INSTRUCTIONS:

1. Preheat oven to 350 degrees.
2. In mixing bowl, cream shortening, sugar, brown sugar, eggs, and milk.
3. In another mixing bowl, combine flour, baking powder, baking soda, and salt. Add to first mixture.
4. Stir in oats, vanilla, and maple flavoring.
5. Drop by teaspoonfuls onto baking sheet. Flatten.
6. Bake for 12 to 15 minutes.

ICING INSTRUCTIONS:

1. In mixing bowl, beat cream cheese, powdered sugar, butter, and some maple flavoring until smooth.
2. If too dry, add splash of water.
3. Spread between 2 cooled cookies.

Emma Yoder, *Clare, MI*

FAVORITE WHOOPIE PIES

COOKIE INGREDIENTS:

2 cups sugar
½ teaspoon salt
1 cup oil
2 teaspoons vanilla
2 eggs
4 cups flour
2 teaspoons baking soda
1 teaspoon baking powder
1 cup cocoa powder
1 cup sour cream
1 cup hot water

FILLING INGREDIENTS:

2 egg whites
1½ cups shortening
2 teaspoons vanilla
4 tablespoons flour
2 tablespoons milk
1 pound powdered sugar (10-X fine)

COOKIE INSTRUCTIONS:

1. Preheat oven to 375 degrees.
2. In bowl, cream together sugar, salt, oil, vanilla, and eggs.
3. In another bowl, sift together flour, baking soda, baking powder, and cocoa powder.
4. Mix sifted ingredients into first mixture alternately with sour cream and hot water.
5. Drop by teaspoonfuls onto baking sheet.
6. Bake for 8 to 10 minutes.
7. When cookies are cooled, spread filling on bottom of 1 cookie and sandwich with another cookie of same size.

FILLING INSTRUCTIONS:

1. In bowl, whip egg whites until foamy.
2. Add shortening, vanilla, flour, milk, and powdered sugar, beating at high speed until light and fluffy.

Ada Stoltzfus, *Loysville, PA*

PUMPKIN WHOOPIE PIES

COOKIE INGREDIENTS:

- 2 cups brown sugar
- 2 cups pumpkin puree
- 1 cup oil
- 2 eggs
- 1 teaspoon cinnamon
- 1 teaspoon salt
- 1 teaspoon baking powder
- 1 teaspoon baking soda
- 2 cups flour

FILLING INGREDIENTS:

- 2 egg whites
- 1½ cups shortening
- 1 pound powdered sugar
- 4 tablespoons flour
- 2 tablespoons milk
- 2 teaspoons vanilla

COOKIE INSTRUCTIONS:

1. Preheat oven to 350 degrees.
2. In large mixing bowl, combine brown sugar, pumpkin, oil, and eggs. Add cinnamon, salt, baking powder, and baking soda. Add flour and mix well.
3. Drop by rounded tablespoonfuls onto parchment-lined baking sheets.
4. Bake for 8 to 10 minutes.
5. Cool completely.

FILLING INSTRUCTIONS:

1. In mixing bowl, beat egg whites until foamy. Add shortening, powdered sugar, flour, milk, and vanilla. Beat on high speed until light and fluffy.
2. Spread between 2 cookies of similar size and shape.

Rachel Stoltzfus, *Loysville, PA*

MONSTER COOKIES

INGREDIENTS:

1 cup butter
1 cup sugar
2 cups brown sugar
6 eggs
3 cups peanut butter
1 teaspoon vanilla
1 teaspoon salt
4 teaspoons baking soda
8 cups quick oats
12 ounces M&M's candies
1 cup raisins (optional)

INSTRUCTIONS:

1. Preheat oven to 350 degrees.
2. In mixing bowl, cream together butter, sugar, and brown sugar. Mix in eggs.
3. Blend in peanut butter, vanilla, salt, and baking soda.
4. Stir in oats until fully moistened.
5. Add M&M's and raisins.
6. Use cookie scoop to drop onto baking sheets.
7. Bake for 12 to 15 minutes. Don't overbake so that they are chewy and not crunchy.

Delila Swartzentruber, *West Salem, OH*

MOLASSES CRINKLES

INGREDIENTS:

1 cup brown sugar
¾ cup shortening
⅓ cup molasses
1 egg
1½ teaspoons baking soda
½ teaspoon salt
1 teaspoon cinnamon
1 teaspoon ground ginger
2¼ cups flour
Powdered sugar

INSTRUCTIONS:

1. Preheat oven to 350 degrees.
2. In mixing bowl, mix brown sugar, shortening, molasses, and egg.
3. Mix in baking soda, salt, cinnamon, and ginger. Add flour until well combined.
4. Chill dough.
5. Roll dough into balls then in powdered sugar. Place on baking sheets.
6. Bake for 12 to 15 minutes. Do not overbake.

Emma Byler, *New Wilmington, PA*

WHITE CHOCOLATE PARTY MIX

A good Christmastime treat.

INGREDIENTS:

- 1 (10 ounce) package mini pretzels
- 5 cups Cheerios cereal
- 5 cups Corn Chex cereal
- 2 cups mixed nuts
- 1 pound M&M's candies
- 2 (12 ounce) packages vanilla baking chips
- 3 tablespoons vegetable oil

INSTRUCTIONS:

1. In large bowl, combine pretzels, Cheerios, Corn Chex, nuts, and M&M's.
2. In microwavable bowl, melt vanilla chips with oil in microwave (or over double boiler) until smooth.
3. Pour over cereal mixture and stir gently to coat well.
4. Spread on waxed paper-lined baking sheets. Cool.
5. Break apart and store in airtight containers.

Mrs. David Byler, *New Castle, PA*

STRAWBERRY PRETZEL SALAD

INGREDIENTS:

2 cups finely crushed pretzels

3 tablespoons sugar

¾ cup butter, melted

1 (8 ounce) package cream cheese

½ cup powdered sugar

1 (8 ounce) carton whipped topping

1 (6 ounce) box strawberry gelatin

2½ cups boiling water

1 (16 ounce) package frozen strawberries

INSTRUCTIONS:

1. Preheat oven to 350 degrees.
2. In bowl, mix pretzels, sugar, and butter. Press into 9x13-inch pan.
3. Bake for 15 minutes. Cool.
4. In bowl, cream together cream cheese and powdered sugar. Fold in whipped topping. Spread over cooled crust.
5. In bowl, dissolve gelatin in boiling water. Stir in strawberries. Chill until slightly thickened.
6. Spread over cream cheese layer. Chill at least 1 hour until firm.

Fannie Ann Byler, *Reynoldsville, PA*

ORANGE CIRCUS PEANUT TAPIOCA

INGREDIENTS:

- 1 pint orange juice
- 1½ quarts water
- ½ teaspoon salt
- 1½ cups tapioca pearls
- 1 large box orange gelatin
- 1 package orange drink mix (like Kool-Aid)
- 1½ cups sugar
- 2 cups chopped circus peanut candies
- 2 cups whipped topping

INSTRUCTIONS:

1. In saucepan, combine orange juice and water; bring to boil. Add salt and tapioca and cook until clear.
2. Remove from heat. Add gelatin, drink mix, sugar, and 1½ cups circus peanuts, stirring until dissolved. Chill.
3. Mix in ½ cup circus peanuts and whipped topping. Chill before serving.

Mrs. Ura Gingerich, *Wellsville, NY*

STOVETOP CUSTARD

INGREDIENTS:

8 eggs
1 quart milk
1 cup sugar
1 teaspoon salt
2 teaspoons vanilla

INSTRUCTIONS:

1. In bowl, beat eggs well. Add milk, sugar, salt, and vanilla. Pour mixture into custard jars.
2. Set jars in saucepan and surround with 1 to 2 inches cold water.
3. Cover and bring water to boil.
4. Remove from heat and let sit for 45 minutes.
5. Refrigerate to fully chill.
6. Good served with fresh berries.

Becky Zook, *Navarre, OH*

24-HOUR HEAVENLY FRUIT SALAD

INGREDIENTS:

3 egg yolks
½ cup sugar
⅓ cup heavy cream
Juice of 1 lemon
1 can crushed pineapple, drained
1 can sweet cherries, drained
1 pound white or red grapes
1 pound mini marshmallows
1 cup whipped cream

INSTRUCTIONS:

1. In medium saucepan, beat together egg yolks, sugar, cream, and lemon juice. Cook over medium heat, stirring until mixture thickens. Be careful not to overcook.
2. Let cool thoroughly.
3. Add drained pineapple and cherries, grapes, and marshmallows, mixing well. Fold in whipped cream.
4. Chill for 24 hours before serving.
5. For variety, sliced bananas and chopped nuts can be added.

Emma Gingerich, *Bremen, OH*

DELICIOUS ICE CREAM

INGREDIENTS:

- 10 cups milk
- 4 tablespoons unflavored gelatin
- 1 cup water
- 8 cups heavy cream
- 12 eggs
- 2 cups maple syrup
- 1 teaspoon stevia
- 2 teaspoons vanilla
- 2 teaspoons maple flavoring

INSTRUCTIONS:

1. In pot, heat 4 cups milk.
2. In bowl, soak gelatin in water and add to milk. Cool.
3. Before it gets too thick, add remaining milk, cream, eggs, maple syrup, stevia, vanilla, and maple flavoring.
4. Pour into 8-quart ice cream freezer.
5. Top with additional milk if needed to fill.
6. Freeze according to manufacturer's directions.

Daniel and Miriam Shetler, *Stanton, MI*

FRUIT SLUSHY

INGREDIENTS:

1½ cups fresh pineapple or 1 (20 ounce) can crushed pineapple
4 cups freshly squeezed orange juice
6 bananas, mashed
2 cups peeled and chopped fresh peaches
1 cup fresh or frozen blueberries (optional)

INSTRUCTIONS:

1. In blender, crush pineapple.
2. In bowl, mix pineapple with orange juice, bananas, peaches, and blueberries. Stir well.
3. Pour into individual freezer containers. Freeze.
4. Partially thaw to enjoy a refreshing treat.

Marian Esh, *Paradise, PA*

MARSHMALLOW ICE CREAM

INGREDIENTS:

1 cup milk
20 marshmallows
1 teaspoon vanilla
1 cup heavy cream

INSTRUCTIONS:

1. In double boiler, heat milk and melt marshmallows. Let mixture cool.
2. Add vanilla.
3. In bowl, whip cream to stiff peaks. Beat in marshmallow mixture.
4. Place in sealable tub in freezer for a few hours until scoopable.
5. Fresh fruit pulp can be folded in for a variety of flavors.

Rachel Yoder, *Fultonville, NY*

PRESERVING *the* HARVEST

He did good, and gave us rain from heaven, and fruitful seasons, filling our hearts with food and gladness.

~ Acts 14:17

YOGURT

INGREDIENTS:

2 tablespoons plain gelatin
1 cup cold water
1 gallon milk
2 cups sugar
1 cup yogurt with active cultures

INSTRUCTIONS:

1. Soak gelatin in cold water.
2. Heat milk to 190 degrees. Cool to 130 degrees.
3. Add sugar, yogurt, and soaked gelatin. Beat with egg beater.
4. Cover and set in a warm place for 4 to 6 hours or until set up. Save 1 cup for next batch.
5. Portion into small containers and chill overnight until fully set.

To flavor: Add 1 can pie filling or 2 boxes flavored gelatin soaked in 2 cups hot water to the batch of yogurt.

Barbara A. Schwartz, *Geneva, IN*

TOMATO COCKTAIL

INGREDIENTS:

¾ bushel tomatoes
1 stalk celery
3 large green peppers
4 large onions
2 cups sugar
Salt and pepper to taste

INSTRUCTIONS:

1. In stockpot, cook tomatoes, celery, green peppers, and onions until soft.
2. Put vegetables through Victorio strainer to remove pulp.
3. To juice, add sugar, salt, and pepper.
4. Ladle juice into quart jars and seal with 2-piece lids.
5. Cold pack for 20 minutes.

Mrs. Menno Miller, *Gallipolis, OH*

BREAD 'N' BUTTER PICKLES

These sold well at our roadside stand.

INGREDIENTS:

- 1 gallon thinly sliced cucumbers
- 8 small onions, sliced
- ½ cup salt
- 5 cups sugar
- 1½ teaspoons turmeric
- 2 tablespoons mustard seed
- 2 cups vinegar
- 2 cups water

INSTRUCTIONS:

1. Place cucumbers and onions in large bowl.
2. Mix in salt and cover with water. Let sit 3 hours.
3. Drain well.
4. In saucepan, combine sugar, turmeric, mustard seed, vinegar, and water. Bring to boil.
5. Remove from heat and mix in cucumbers and onions.
6. Ladle into pint jars and seal with 2-piece lids.
7. Cold pack for 10 minutes.

Mrs. Monroe Miller, *Blanchard, MI*

PICKLED RED BEETS

INGREDIENTS:

- 2 gallons red beets
- 8 cups sugar
- 1 cup strong vinegar
- 1½ cups water
- 2 tablespoons salt

INSTRUCTIONS:

1. In kettle, cover beets in water and cook until soft.
2. Remove skins and cut into chunks. Reserve cooking water.
3. In saucepan, combine 2 cups beet cooking water, sugar, vinegar, water, and salt. Bring to boil.
4. Pack beets into canning jars. Fill jars with hot syrup.
5. Cold pack for 10 minutes to seal.

Amanda Zook, *Dalton, OH*

KOSHER DILL PICKLES

INGREDIENTS:

- 9 cups sugar
- 9 cups water
- 3 cups vinegar
- 3 tablespoons kosher dill mix
- 1 tablespoon salt
- 1 tablespoon turmeric
- Pickles or small cucumbers
- Small onions

INSTRUCTIONS:

1. In large saucepan, combine sugar, water, vinegar, dill mix, and salt and bring to boil.
2. Slice pickles and pack into canning jars. Add thick slice of onion to top of each jar.
3. Pour syrup over top.
4. Cold pack jars for 5 minutes.

Sara Miller, *Fredericksburg, OH*

WATERMELON RIND PICKLES

INGREDIENTS:

- 2 quarts cold water
- 1 tablespoon lime juice
- 4 pounds watermelon rind, peeled and cut into 1-inch squares
- 2 tablespoons whole allspice
- 2 tablespoons whole cloves
- 10 (2 inch) sticks cinnamon
- 1 quart vinegar
- 1 quart water
- 4 pounds sugar

INSTRUCTIONS:

1. Combine 2 quarts water and lime and pour over watermelon rind. Let stand 1 hour.
2. Drain, place in stockpot, and cover rind with cold water. Heat and simmer 1½ hours or until tender.
3. Drain.
4. Tie allspice, cloves, and cinnamon in cheesecloth.
5. In kettle, combine vinegar, 1 quart water, and sugar, heating until sugar dissolves.
6. Add spice bag and watermelon rind. Simmer gently for 2 hours.
7. Pack rind in sterilized pint jars and fill jars with hot syrup.
8. Seal in hot water bath for 8 minutes.

Makes 6 pints.

Marty and Laura Miller, *Greenfield, OH*

SLICED SWEET PICKLES

INGREDIENTS:

2 gallons sliced cucumbers
2 cups salt
1 rounded tablespoon alum
1½ quarts water
½ quart vinegar
14 cups sugar
2 tablespoons mixed pickling spice
1 teaspoon turmeric
1 teaspoon celery seed

INSTRUCTIONS:

1. In large container, cover cucumbers in cold water and add salt. Let sit for 4 days.
2. Drain cold water then cover with boiling water. Let stand for 12 to 24 hours.
3. Drain and cover with hot water that has alum dissolved in it. Let sit 24 hours.
4. Drain and rinse well with cold water.
5. In saucepan, combine 1½ quarts water, vinegar, sugar, pickling spice, turmeric, and celery seed. Bring to boil, stirring to dissolve sugar. Pour over cucumbers.
6. Each day for 3 days, drain syrup off and reheat syrup. Then pour it back over cucumbers.
7. Pack cucumbers in canning jars and fill jars with syrup.
8. Cold pack until just boiling to seal.

Susan L. Gingerich, *Dalton, OH*

MIXED PICKLES

INGREDIENTS:

- 1½ quarts fresh green beans
- 3 quarts mini corn cobs
- 2 quarts chopped celery
- 9 quarts chopped onion
- 2 bags baby carrots
- 3 heads cauliflower, separated
- 6 bell peppers of any color, chopped
- 2 to 3 quarts small pickles or cucumbers
- 5 (16 ounce) cans butter beans, drained and rinsed
- 5 (16 ounce) cans dark red kidney beans, drained and rinsed
- 7 cups white vinegar
- 2 cups apple cider vinegar
- 8 cups water
- 10½ cups sugar

INSTRUCTIONS:

1. Cook all fresh vegetables separately in salted water until softened.
2. Drain and combine vegetables in large container. Add beans.
3. In large bowl, mix white vinegar, apple cider vinegar, water, and sugar until sugar is dissolved.
4. Pack mixed vegetables into quart canning jars.
5. Pour brine over vegetables to fill jars.
6. Cold pack for 15 minutes to seal.

Emma Yoder, *Clare, MI*

SANDWICH SPREAD

INGREDIENTS:

- 6 large onions
- 6 large cucumbers
- 6 green peppers
- 6 red peppers
- 1 handful salt
- 2 cups apple cider vinegar
- 1 heaping cup flour
- ½ quart mustard
- ½ quart salad dressing
- 1 tablespoon turmeric
- 1 tablespoon vinegar
- 5 cups sugar

INSTRUCTIONS:

1. Chop onions, cucumbers, green peppers, and red peppers.
2. Mix with salt and place in colander for 1 hour to drain.
3. Place vegetables in stockpot and bring to boil for 15 minutes.
4. Add apple cider vinegar.
5. In bowl, mix flour, mustard, salad dressing, turmeric, vinegar, and sugar.
6. Add to boiling mixture and boil for 5 minutes.
7. Ladle into pint canning jars and seal with 2-piece lids.
8. Seal in hot water bath for 10 minutes.

Kristina Mast, *New Holstein, WI*

DELICIOUS SALSA

INGREDIENTS:

- 16 cups peeled and diced tomatoes
- 4 large onions, chopped
- ¼ to ½ cup chopped hot peppers
- 2 cups chopped green pepper
- 4 (6 ounce) cans tomato paste
- ¾ cup vinegar
- 1 cup sugar
- 1 teaspoon basil
- 1 tablespoon garlic salt
- 1 tablespoon parsley flakes
- 1 tablespoon salt
- 1 teaspoon pepper

INSTRUCTIONS:

1. Combine all ingredients in large kettle and simmer for 30 to 60 minutes.
2. Ladle into hot jars and cold pack for 30 minutes.
3. Make sure you have a bag of tortilla chips handy to taste test and enjoy.

Lizzie Ann Swartzentruber,
Newcomerstown, OH

HOT PEPPERS

INGREDIENTS:

1 clove garlic
1 teaspoon salt
Pinch alum
Hot peppers, sliced
½ teaspoon oregano
1 teaspoon vegetable oil
1 quart white vinegar
1 quart water
3 cups sugar

INSTRUCTIONS:

1. To each pint jar add 1 clove garlic, 1 teaspoon salt, and pinch alum.
2. Fill jar with sliced hot peppers and top with ½ teaspoon oregano and 1 teaspoon oil.
3. In saucepan, combine vinegar, water, and sugar. Bring to boil and stir to dissolve sugar.
4. Pour into jars to cover peppers.
5. Seal jars in hot water bath for 5 minutes.

Susan Byler, *Atlantic, PA*

BEST BBQ SAUCE

INGREDIENTS:

- 15 cups thick and pulpy tomato juice
- 2 cups blended onion
- ¾ cup with half lemon and half lime juice
- ⅔ cup sugar
- 9 cups brown sugar
- 1¾ cups apple cider vinegar
- ⅔ cup prepared mustard
- 2 cups Worcestershire sauce
- ⅔ cup liquid smoke
- ⅓ cup paprika
- ½ cup salt
- 1 tablespoon garlic salt
- 1½ cups Therm Flo

INSTRUCTIONS:

1. In kettle, combine 13 cups tomato juice, blended onion, lemon and lime juice, sugar, brown sugar, vinegar, mustard, Worcestershire sauce, liquid smoke, paprika, salt, and garlic salt. Bring to slow boil for 1 hour.
2. In bowl, make paste of Therm Flo and 2 cups tomato juice. Whisk into hot sauce to thicken. Blending in blender or with submersion blender for few seconds makes sauce smooth.
3. Ladle into canning jars and seal with 2-piece lids.
4. Seal in hot water bath for 20 minutes.

Becky Fisher, *Lancaster, PA*

CREAM SOUP MIX

INGREDIENTS:

- 2 cups instant dry milk
- ¾ cup cornstarch
- ¼ cup chicken bouillon
- 2 tablespoons onion flakes or powder
- 2 teaspoons seasoned salt
- ¼ teaspoon pepper

INSTRUCTIONS:

1. Mix all ingredients together well.
2. Store in airtight container.
3. To use: Mix ⅓ cup soup mix with 1 cup cold water. Heat in saucepan over low heat until it boils and thickens. If you want more flavor, dice up some celery or mushrooms and add while cooking. Equals 1 can undiluted cream soup.

Emma Byler, *New Wilmington, PA*

PEANUT BUTTER SPREAD

This spread is commonly served and even sold in Amish restaurants.

INGREDIENTS:

- 10 cups brown sugar
- 5 cups water
- ¾ cup corn syrup
- 5 pounds creamy peanut butter
- 3 quarts marshmallow fluff
- 1 teaspoon maple flavoring

INSTRUCTIONS:

1. In saucepan, combine brown sugar, water, and corn syrup; bring to boil for 5 to 10 minutes.
2. Cool slightly. Add peanut butter and marshmallow fluff, stirring until nice and fluffy. Add maple flavoring.

Mattie J. Gingerich, *Dalton, OH*

STRAWBERRY FREEZER JAM

This is my husband's favorite of all jams to eat with fresh bread and homemade butter.

INGREDIENTS:

- 4 cups sugar
- 2 cups crushed strawberries
- 5 level tablespoons Sure-Jell
- ¾ cup water

INSTRUCTIONS:

1. In bowl, mix sugar and strawberries. Let stand for 10 minutes.
2. Meanwhile, in saucepan, mix Sure-Jell into water and cook for 1 minute.
3. Add Sure-Jell to strawberries. Keep at room temperature for 24 hours.
4. Refrigerate or freeze.

Raymond and Miriam Troyer, *Blanchard, MI*

STRAWBERRY-RHUBARB JELLY

INGREDIENTS:

- 5 cups finely chopped rhubarb
- 5 cups sugar
- 2 cups crushed pineapple
- 1 (6 ounce) package strawberry gelatin

INSTRUCTIONS:

1. Combine rhubarb, sugar, and pineapple and let sit overnight.
2. In morning, bring mixture to boil and cook about 20 minutes until tender.
3. Remove from heat and add gelatin, stirring until dissolved.
4. Portion into containers. Refrigerate or freeze.

Mrs. Lizzie Schwartz, *Geneva, IN*

ZUCCHINI-APRICOT JAM

INGREDIENTS:

- 6 cups peeled and grated zucchini
- 6 cups sugar
- ¾ cup crushed pineapple with juice
- ½ cup lemon juice
- 6 ounces apricot gelatin

INSTRUCTIONS:

1. In large saucepan, combine zucchini and sugar. Cook over low heat until sugar is dissolved. Bring to boil for 15 minutes.
2. Add pineapple and lemon juice. Boil 6 minutes.
3. Remove from heat and mix in gelatin.
4. Pour into jelly jars and seal with 2-piece lids.
5. Cold pack for 5 minutes.

Susan L. Gingerich, *Dalton, OH*

BLACKBERRY PIE FILLING

INGREDIENTS:

- 8 cups fresh blackberries
- 12 cups water
- 4½ cups sugar
- 2 cups Therm Flo or Perma Flo

INSTRUCTIONS:

1. In stockpot, boil blackberries and water for 10 minutes. Stir in sugar.
2. Wisk in Therm Flo until thick.
3. Pour into quart canning jars. Seal with 2-piece lids.
4. Cold pack for 10 minutes.

Esther and John Schwartz, *Kentucky*

BLACKBERRY CRUMBLE DESSERT

INGREDIENTS:

1 quart jar blackberry pie filling

½ cup flour

⅓ cup sugar

4 tablespoons butter

INSTRUCTIONS:

1. Preheat oven to 375 degrees.
2. Pour pie filling into 2-quart baking dish.
3. In bowl, combine flour, sugar, and butter with fork until crumbly; spread over pie filling.
4. Bake 30 to 40 minutes until bubbling.

Esther and John Schwartz, *Kentucky*

INDEX OF CONTRIBUTORS

INDEX OF RECIPES BY SECTION

Breaking the Fast

Rolling the Dough

Nourishing the Family

Adding to the Feast

Satisfying the Sweet Tooth

Preserving the Harvest

INDEX OF RECIPES BY KEY INGREDIENTS

Pumpkin

Raisins

Rice

Rhubarb

Sour Cream

Strawberries

Sweet Potatoes

Tapioca